The Offensive Coordinator's Football Handbook

Steve Axman

ISBN: 978-1-60679-466-1
Library of Congress Control Number: 2019941038
Cover design: Cheery Sugabo
Book layout: Cheery Sugabo
Front cover photo: © Shane Roper/CSM via ZUMA Wire

Coaches Choice
P.O. Box 1828
Monterey, CA 93942
www.coacheschoice.com

Dedication

Once again, to my

wonderful wife

and best buddy!

Dr. Marie L. Axman

and

To my good friend

Dr. Jim Peterson

of Coaches Choice, who

has kept my writing

hobby going for many a

year.

Acknowledgments

With any acknowledgment, I must start out with my two greatest mentors, Homer Smith and Larry Smith. Homer taught me about offensive design and strategy, which became my own knowledge foundation for on-the-field, offensive football. Larry taught me much about program leadership and management. I am so grateful and appreciative to have been under their teaching wings.

Keith Gilbertson also had a big impact on me in regard to game-planning and play calling. Together, we both worked hard and had a tremendous amount of fun doing so. I am extremely grateful for all of the help I've received over the years to have been able to develop and write a book such as *The Offensive Coordinator's Football Handbook*. Thanks to Joe Scannella, Dom Anile, Denny Douds, Bob Ford, Bruce Tarbox, Frank Gibson, Willie Peete, Lindy Infante, Gary Moeller, Mouse Davis, June Jones, Jack Elway, Dave Baldwin, Steve Kragthorpe, Ken Zampese, Marty Mornhinweg, Steve Loney, Ed Kezarian, Johnathan Smith, Charlie Dickey, and Dan Finn. These are a few of the many individuals who have been a great help to me, whether they realize it or not. Thanks also goes to Preston Jones, Adam Schiermyer, and Chance Clatterbush for their assistance. Special thanks goes to my three "...go-to..." guys and great friends Gary Bernardi, Ted Williams, and Brent Myers.

Special thanks to my wife, Marie, my sons-in-law Ross Grainger and Chris Schuld, as well as Coach Donte Bartee for their assistance, when my sketchy computer skills came dangerously close to totally blowing up the manuscript a good number of times.

Contents

Introduction

The Joys and Tribulations of Being an Offensive Coordinator

I must start out the writing of *The Offensive Coordinator's Football Handbook* by saying that my numerous years of coaching as an offensive coordinator has helped produce a tremendous amount of pride, enjoyment, and fulfillment throughout my football coaching career. I have greatly enjoyed designing offenses and fitting the players I had at hand into positions where they could be the most productive. I have loved the structuring and planning of our offensive designs against opponents. I have taken great pleasure in the teaching and practicing of those offensive attacks, as our staff worked their tails off to help the players be all they were capable of being. I have savored the constant, everyday comradery with my staffs. I have also delighted in working with the young men who were our players, be they offensive, defensive, special teams, or scout players.

Game-day is…well…game-day! Without a doubt, game-day is one of the most exciting and thrilling aspects that an offensive coordinator and his staff and players can experience. When you win, you are able to cherish moments in time that you can joyously share with your head coach, the assistant coaches, the offensive players, and the entire team. When you lose, you get the chance to get up off the ground, dust yourself off, learn from your mistakes, and fix what needs fixing.

I have been very fortunate to have had the opportunity to coach in programs that have allowed me a full, or almost full, reign on the type of offense we utilized and on how we have executed those specific offensive designs. This freedom allowed me and the many fine offensive staff coaches with whom I have worked to be extremely productive. It allowed our offensive to do our part in helping to be successful and in the helping of our team…our program, win!

Unfortunately, I have also coached in a program where I did not have the control I felt I needed to help make our offense successful in our efforts to help our team…our program, win. I must say that if an offensive coordinator or a coach, in general, coaches long enough, he probably will meet situations where he fails to meet set, established goals, as per the program's or head coach's desire. Fortunately, for me, that only happened once during my career, and I was amicably able to lick my wounds, learn from the experience, and move on. If a coordinator or coach coaches long enough, I am sure that somewhere along the line, he will, unfortunately, find himself in such a similar challenging situation.

Win or lose…good or bad, it is the challenge…the test to see, over the course of years, just how well you, as the offensive coordinator, can manage and guide the people under your charge to help you to become a dynamically successful offensive coordinator. Hopefully, reading *The Offensive Coordinator's Football Handbook* will be a valuable assistance to you in that quest.

CHAPTER 1
BEING AN OFFENSIVE COORDINATOR

It is extremely important for a potential offensive coordinator to clearly and specifically understand what his role will be as a team's offensive coordinator. The underlying basis of this statement is to help a coordinator, or would-be coordinator, be sure that he is fully aware of his role as that team's offensive coordinator, as designated by the head coach. Without question, the best time to do this is before the would-be offensive coordinator accepts the all-important position. In other words, it is essential that he knows what he is getting into when he accepts the position.

For argument's sake, let's say that you've just been named the offensive coordinator for your school's football program. Or, you've just been hired by another school in your league, where you are to become that team's new offensive coordinator. Whatever the reason for the offensive coordinator position scenario, it is important to be aware that the role of being a team's offensive coordinator can differ greatly from team to team.

What a football coach who desires to be an offensive coordinator must understand from the get-go is for what, exactly, is he going to be responsible. He must clearly and specifically understand what will be the roles and goals he must fulfill to be deemed successful by his head coach at the end of the season. The expectations of an offense loaded with talented, upper-classmen could, and should, be higher than an offense loaded with underclassmen, having a virtual lack of varsity experience. Arguably, most people, including you, would undoubtedly agree with such a statement. On the other hand, with your formidable desire to be a successful offensive coordinator … would you?

The Offensive Coordinator's Position

In general, the job …the role …the underlying objective of an offensive coordinator's position is to organize, direct, manage, and lead all of the work efforts of his offensive staff, the offensive players, and, possibly, any athletic department support staff under his charge. On the other hand, it is essential for the offensive coordinator to fully realize that the head coach is still the boss. As a result, the head coach may want to draw up the weekly game plan or, even, to design the structure of the offense. The head coach may also want to dictate what run or pass plays he wants practiced for third-down, red zone, or goal line offense during specific team practice period segments against the scout squad. Come game time, the head coach may even want to be the person calling the offensive plays, instead of the designated offensive coordinator.

In other words, an offensive coordinator may have full control over the total operation—teaching, coaching, and designing the offense, or, he may take on the role of a facilitator of the offense, making sure everything that the head coach wants for each and every game plan is well prepared and practiced. Of course, there's also always the possibility of working at a school that is in between both of those two scenarios, with regard to what will be the true role of the offensive coordinator.

What becomes important, at this point, is that the offensive coordinator can, enthusiastically, functionally, and comfortably, fit into his assigned roles as the offensive coordinator, as per the head coach's directions. This factor would be true whether the offensive coordinator is fully in command of the offense or not. If the attitude of the offensive coordinator is a byproduct of frustration and disbelief, because of his feelings that he, himself, is being held back in his efforts to produce a successful offense, it might be the time for that individual to turn the offensive coordinator position down and look for another job.

CHAPTER 2
PUTTING TOGETHER AN OFFENSIVE COACHING STAFF

As the offensive coordinator, putting together your offensive staff, at this point, should be your first priority. That concern is true, if you are a new offensive coordinator with a full staff of offensive coaches to hire or a veteran offensive coordinator with only one coaching opening on his staff to fill. In reality, the head coach might be the person who handles the search. Even if the head coach is in the forefront of hiring all of his staff members, however, the offensive coordinator should be extensively included in the search, whenever possible. Of course, the head coach is the individual who will, normally, make hiring decisions on his staff. On the other hand, it is important for the offensive coordinator to be actively involved in making decisions concerning offensive staff to help create a cohesive, functional group.

Putting together a staff, you might say, is a little farfetched for your situation. To accept the coordinator's position, you might have to accept the assistant coaches who are already in place, especially if they are fulltime teachers, by order of the athletic director or principal. However, when an offensive coordinator is tasked to find assistants to help fill his staff, he should start by analyzing just what type of coach he feels he needs to best fill the coaching void that currently exists.

What Type of Assistant Coaches Are Needed?

It is difficult for a new offensive coordinator to fill any vacancies he may have on his staff until he does a complete and thorough analysis of what type of coaches he may be, or will be, inheriting. Complete and thorough are key words in the effort to make, and finalize, such important decisions. There are, almost always, candidates who seem to be no-brainers—coaches who clearly should be retained on the new staff. One of your first thoughts in this situation, however, should be why does such a coach seem to be such an easy person to pick as a member of the staff? Is it because he is a great guy? … a fun guy? … a popular coach with the returning coaches and players?

The aforementioned qualities can be very important with regard to the chemistry of a coaching staff. On the other hand, there are several other extremely important reasons to decide on when hiring a coach, besides smiles and being a good guy. Now, don't get the point being made wrong. Being a good person with good character, a pleasant demeanor, and sound, solid values should be a paramount part of the decision-making process.

There certainly are some other basic coaching qualities, however, that are also extremely important when considering the hiring of a coach. For example, you need coaches to fill the vacancies who can help produce a sound, solid coaching staff. You also need people who can blend well together with the present staff to form the type of personal chemistry that can help your offense to be cohesive and consistently effective.

In reality, hiring a quality person to be a coach on your staff should be a prime consideration for you. Personally, I have always felt that that was an extremely important requirement for any of the coaching candidates I decided to interview. Loyalty, honesty, and concern for the well-being of others should all be must factors for any candidate. Teaching and coaching skills are two of the other key concerns you want to know about from the people seated in front of you being interviewed.

The bottom line is that good coaching is good teaching. If a person cannot teach, it's going to be very difficult to be a good coach. Good, solid, veteran coaches who meet many, if not all, of these highly desired coaching qualities should be the coaches who make up most of your staff. This factor is especially true if you are taking over a new offensive coordinator's position yourself.

Figuring Out What Type of Assistant Coaches Are Needed

Figuring out what you need to best fill your offensive staff can, actually, be quite a chore. At the least, it is much more of a chore than you might otherwise think. If you need an offensive line coach, then you need to find an offensive line coach who best fits the bill for you and your offense with regard to attitude, coaching ability, flexibility, experience, work ethic, and offensive line football knowledge. If you are a triple option coach, of some sort, it would probably best for you to look for and consider an offensive line coach who has an appropriate amount of experience coaching option football. On the other hand, if you are a pass-oriented coach, you should probably focus on a pass-blocking coach. Keep in mind, however, that good coaches find a way to coach well amidst any type of offensive design. When in doubt, pick the stronger coach.

Personally, I've always preferred hiring fiery coaches who seemed to have chips on their shoulders, with regard to the performance of their players. Furthermore, I've wanted to sense a feeling of a love of the game and a love for coaching in the members of my staff. I have heard myself say many, many times over the years how lucky I have been to be able to be paid to do what I felt was my hobby—coaching football. Don't get me wrong, however. The coaching life can be a tough one, especially for a coach who has a family. In my coaching career, I have moved my family well over 20 times from the east coast to the west coast and back and forth again.

All factors considered, the more experienced your offensive coaching staff, the better will be your chances to help your offensive players to self-actualize and be all they are capable of being. On the other hand, the personality and communicative skills of a good assistant coach are equally important to me. Quite simply, I want to enjoy the people with whom I work on a daily basis. Yes, I want aggressive, firm, tough-minded assistant coaches. I also, however, want assistant coaches who are great teachers and communicators and have a sincere concern for the well-being of the players as people, as opposed to being coaches who are yellers and screamers.

Putting Together a Balanced Staff

When I coached at the University of Arizona, I was taught by the Wildcats head coach, Larry Smith, that when putting together a staff, you need a combination of wizened, self-assured, older veteran coaches, with fiery, newbie, young-buck coaches, as well as a few coaches who are somewhere in between those two classifications. Larry's underlying thought process was to produce a well-coordinated balance of the coaching experiences on any of the offensive, defensive, or special teams sides of the football. Over the years, his thinking has been a tremendously valued guideline for me in my coaching career, as an offensive coordinator and as a head coach.

I have also strongly come to believe that great coaches are great teachers. As such, these coaches can come in all shapes and forms … young, old, fiery, stoic, experienced, or inexperienced. It is the job of the head coach and the coordinators to find the right combinations of people to best help facilitate the teaching and coaching efforts of the players at hand.

Throughout my coaching career, I was fortunate to have been able to surround myself with such balances of coaching staff members. When hiring young or old, veterans or newbies, I wanted to be sure that when I was holding interviews, I felt it quite important to me to sense that the coaching candidate being interviewed before me seemed to be the kind of person who was sitting on the edge of his seat ready to explode, if he didn't get offered the coaching position. In that regard, it was extremely important for me to sense a strong desire to become a part of our football program from any of the candidates I was considering.

What If a Specific Coach Can't Be Found?

Another concern a coordinator might have in successfully attempting to put together a balanced, quality offensive staff is what would he do, if he couldn't find that specific offensive line, quarterback, running back, tight end, or wide receiver coach whom he believes he needs? Arguably, there are numerous candidates available for almost every assistant coaching position. The key issue is to find the right assistant coach for the vacant position on your staff.

In my career, when I couldn't find the right offensive line coach to complete our staff, I would take a different route. I would hire a person whom I felt was a great offensive coach of some sort and make him the offensive line coach. I would be sure that the person was a coach who would treat this situation as a great challenge … a tremendous opportunity … a great way to grow in the coaching profession. The result of such an action to fill my staff was always extremely positive. I never once was disappointed in undertaking such a hiring strategy.

CHAPTER 3
UTILIZING THE VOLUNTEER COACH

On the high school, junior college, and smaller college levels, it has become quite common to utilize volunteer coaches to help fulfill offensive assistant coaching positions. There are many individuals who are excited about the possibility of helping to coach on a volunteer, non-pay status. Volunteer coaches can come to you in all shapes and forms.

If you ask my wife, she'll tell you I'm retired from football coaching. I say out of work. For the 2016 football season, I volunteered at Perry High School in Gilbert, Arizona, a local high school that is a few miles from my house. I felt that with well over 40 years of football coaching experience, I still had much to offer as a volunteer coach. Another of our school's volunteer coaches, who assists the offensive line coach, has 12 years of NFL playing experience. Why do we, as volunteer football coaches, do this? Quite simply, we volunteer because we want to remain a part of the great game of football, a game we love so much.

Almost all high schools have some set guidelines with regard to the number of paid assistant coaches they can have, whether from the school's faculty or from off-campus personnel. As a rule, there always seems to be a coach or two, however, who is willing to coach for no financial consideration at all. Furthermore, some of these volunteer coaches are as good a coach as any of the paid coaches on the staff. Why? Because, they love the game of football. They also love coaching football. In fact, they may have many years of coaching experience under their belts to share. They love working with young people. They love to see young football players grow and develop under their guidance. In addition, they love the action and interaction inherent in practice, the staff meetings, and the Friday or Saturday games.

Keys for Utilizing Volunteer Coaches

The basic keys for utilizing volunteer coaches is, first of all, that such volunteers can be counted on to be consistent attendance-wise in their commitment to help coach the team. On the other hand, the use of an offensive volunteer coach might be set up in a fashion that the volunteer coach might be able to only donate his volunteer coaching time for two afternoons a week. Hopefully, those two volunteer days would be for the two heavy practice days of a team's practice. It is one thing for a volunteer to try to be consistently available for whatever the agreement is with regard to actual coaching participation. It is another matter for problems to arise with regard to consistent, pre-arranged coaching participation. For a volunteer coach to be inconsistent in his ability to carry out responsibilities by missing practices is, frankly, disconcerting for the offensive coordinator, the assistant coaches, and the players.

As a rule, it is best to have volunteers work as assistants to the assistant coaches. In this manner, the volunteer coaches can be a tremendous asset to the coordinator and the offense whenever they possibly can, without being disturbing to the coaching flow of the offense when they can't. On the other hand, if a volunteer can be at practice every day without complications, the staff can become that much more enhanced. A consistent, volunteer coaching program must be worked out by the coordinator and/ or head coach to insure that inabilities to consistently help as a volunteer does not become a problem.

The second major key, or concern, with regard to the utilization of volunteer coaches is to make sure that such volunteers have enough football background to be able to adequately act as assistant coaches. There are a lot of ex-football players who can make excellent volunteer assistant coaches due to their playing experience. However, playing and coaching are two different issues. When utilizing volunteer assistant coaches, the offensive coordinator must be sure to properly bring such volunteer assistants "… up-to-snuff …" with regard to the offense being utilized, the requirements of the techniques of the position that the volunteer coach will be coaching and the actual teaching and drilling of the techniques and assignments that the players must master. If there are a number of such volunteer coaches, it might be best to have such volunteers work with some of the fulltime assistant coaches, who can act as mentor coaches to them.

Soliciting Volunteer Assistants

Where can a coordinator find such volunteer assistant coach help? Maybe the coordinator solicits a fellow, on-campus teacher. Perhaps the coordinator convinces one of the on-campus security officers to become a volunteer assistant. Maybe there's a parent of one of his players who not only has the requisite skill-set, but is also able to arrange his work schedule who would like to volunteer. On the other hand, perhaps a local businessman or team booster has the free time to volunteer coach and help coach your offense.

The offensive coordinator must be careful, however, when utilizing friends, especially if they actually have minimal football coaching experience. You don't need people hanging around the football office with little football experience and with little, or nothing to do. If someone is willing to volunteer, it's your job as the offensive coordinator to make sure that such volunteers have meaningful, necessary roles and assignments.

Once you assign someone to a volunteer coaching position, it's your responsibility, as the offensive coordinator, to make sure the volunteer coaches truly know what they're supposed to do and that they are able to execute their coaching roles effectively. In essence, the offensive coordinator needs to coach the coaches on his staff, whether his assistant coaches are paid full-time, part-time, or volunteer coaches.

Grooming the Young Volunteer Coach

Successful, young, inexperienced volunteer coaches have always been a tremendous source of interest for me. Some young, volunteer coaches will coach for a season and realize the world of football coaching is not for them. That's OK. At a minimum, they will not go through life wondering if they should have tried to go into football coaching.

I have greatly enjoyed working with young, volunteer coaches whom I would quickly see catch fire, work hard to become a good coaches, and quickly succeed at doing so. These are the coaches who would quickly become the low-on-the-totem pole, young-buck, unpaid coaches on your offensive or defensive staff. I, myself, started out as a volunteer coach at Freeport High School in Freeport, New York and quickly climbed the volunteer ladder to being a full-paid assistant coach the next year.

When young, ex-football players ask me how they can get into the football coaching profession, I tell them to volunteer at the highest level of football coaching possible. Why? Because the head coach or offensive coordinator can quickly spot the talented volunteers and want them to be on their staff when an opening occurs at that higher level of play. On the other hand, the head coach or offensive coordinator might move on to a new position at another school's football program and might want to take that young volunteer coach with him as a part- or full-time coach on his new staff.

I don't want to imply that relatively young coaches who want to get into the world of football coaching should necessarily have an ambition to coach on the college level or at a high level of high school varsity or junior varsity competition. A young volunteer might be most interested in assisting freshman high school football and end up happily coaching at such a level for years, either as a volunteer or as a paid assistant.

CHAPTER 4
RESEARCHING THE OFFENSE

The word or term "… design …" is often used in this book with regard to your total offensive package to help instill creativity, soundness, and balance in your system. At this stage of the game, you should think of yourself as both a researcher and an architect. The architect aspect sounds like it would be more fun to me. Scribbling out sheets of run and pass plays, with possible varieties of personnel plans, formations, shifts, and motions can be an absolutely challenging and fulfilling project. On the other hand, similar to writing that college term paper years ago, a research term paper must focus, initially, on the word "research." Chapter 4 features a smorgasbord of ideas and concepts to help provide you with thoughts that you can utilize to help you to research the information you need to properly create the offense … the offensive design … the offensive package you want and feel that you need.

Start Out Creating the Offense by Brainstorming

You may very well have it in your mind that you want to utilize a spread passing offense, for example. Fine! At this point, you should sink your teeth into researching everything you can find on the spread passing offense. You might start out by calling some of your coaching colleagues who are not in your conference, whose teams presently employ the spread passing offense. Meet with those friends. Let them clinic you on their version of the spread passing offense.

As you start to get a good understanding of the basic concepts of their offenses, be sure to ask the tough questions, as well as the basic questions, concerning their version of the spread passing offense. No offensive structure is perfect. So, be sure to ask your coaching colleagues what the strengths are of the spread passing offense that their teams utilize. In turn, also inquire into the weaknesses of their particular scheme. What makes it tick? Why do they use separate versions of the spread offense? You suddenly remember that another of your coaching friends was using the spread passing offense for the last few years but dropped it after this past season. Why did he make such a change?

A local college is using the spread passing offense. Due to recruiting, and in-state loyalties, there's a good chance that such a college's or university's football staff will kindly discus their version of the spread offense with you. You should also consider driving to the next state that also has a college using the spread offense. Try to make it to their spring game or at least to a few of their spring practices. Make appointments ahead of time to speak to their coaches. Another viable possibility is to specifically attend one or more state, city, or privately conducted clinics, where certain coaches are scheduled to speak on the spread passing offense.

You should also check on the availability of instructional books, articles, and video tapes concerning the spread passing offense. Analyze what they have to say. Get on YouTube to check out any talks on the spread passing offense. There's a relatively good chance that you played a team or two, or even three, which used some version of the spread passing offense. Study their video tapes. Either get on Hudl or find other videotape and study why teams were effective or why they weren't, when running the spread passing offense. Research, research, and research, until you feel you're repeating the information gained from your research. Once you have accomplished this, you're now in the ballpark of the knowledge you'll need concerning the offense … the offensive design you want to create for your own team.

The Coordinator Shouldn't Do All of the Research Himself

A key to such a project for an offensive coordinator is to be sure that the offensive coordinator uses his assistant coaches to help in the overall research project. For an offensive coordinator to try to research all of the aforementioned information by himself would be a massive and time-consuming undertaking. That's why a coordinator should assign parts of the total spread passing offense study, or whatever offensive package the coordinator wants to research, to the individual members of his offensive staff.

Such shared work projects give the assistants an important stake in the creation of the offense to be utilized, which helps to produce an ownership in the shared, offensive design that is developed. For example, in the sharing of the offensive design workload, the offensive line coach could do an analysis of the pass protections employed in a spread passing offense. In turn, the running back coach might be assigned to evaluate the run game in a spread passing offense. The wide receiver coach could be given responsibility for determining the variety of pass patterns and pass routes used by the backs, tight ends, and wide receivers in such a system. The coordinator himself, could focus in on formation, motion, and shifting actions used in a spread passing offense, as well as possibly third-down offense and red zone offense. One way or the other, a total verbal and written analysis should be presented by the entire offensive staff to present a unified study of offensive designs, such as the spread passing offense, the wishbone offense, the spread read-option offense, the I-option offense, the wing-T, or any other offensive system that a team may have interest in studying and utilizing.

Package the Separate Parts of the Offense

A series of runs, run options, play-action passes, dropback, and, possibly, sprint-out or move-out passes must be designed to complement the potential effectiveness of the various elements of the offense. For example, a zone run play-based offense should contain an inside zone and, possibly, an outside zone run play. The inside zone is a quick-hitting inside run play. In turn, an outside zone run play is a stretch run play to the wide side. Both the inside and the outside zone run play should, in my opinion, be augmented by a counter run play, back away from the side of the inside and outside zone run-play actions. These three, packaged, zone run play-actions are detailed in Diagram 4-1.

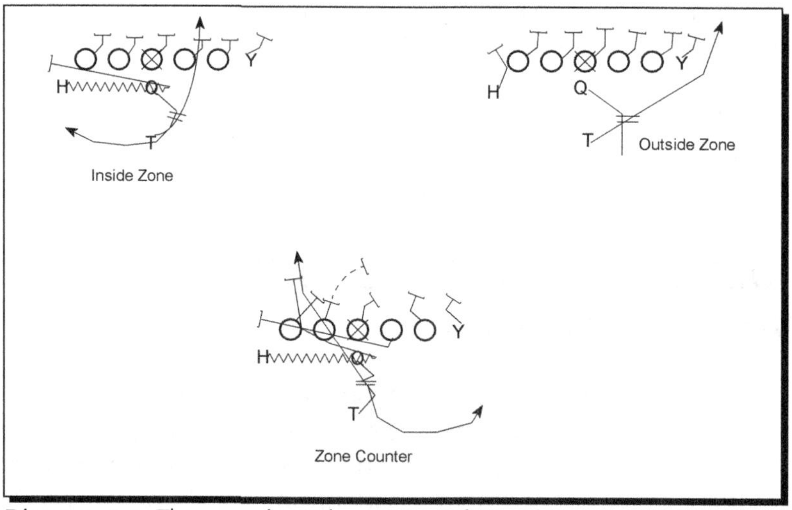

Diagram 4-1. Three packaged zone run play-actions

Another must in your effort to create a well-supported zone run game package is to utilize a naked (bootleg) pass play, which can act both as a zone counter run play (quarterback run-keep action) and as a zone counter play-action passes. In addition, quick plays (three-step timed, play-action passes) can be developed off of an inside zone run play to help quickly attack a defense's linebacker and secondary coverage efforts. In addition, deeper thrown play-action passes can be thrown off of slower developing outside zone run plays. These three complementary zone play-action passes are illustrated in Diagram 4-2.

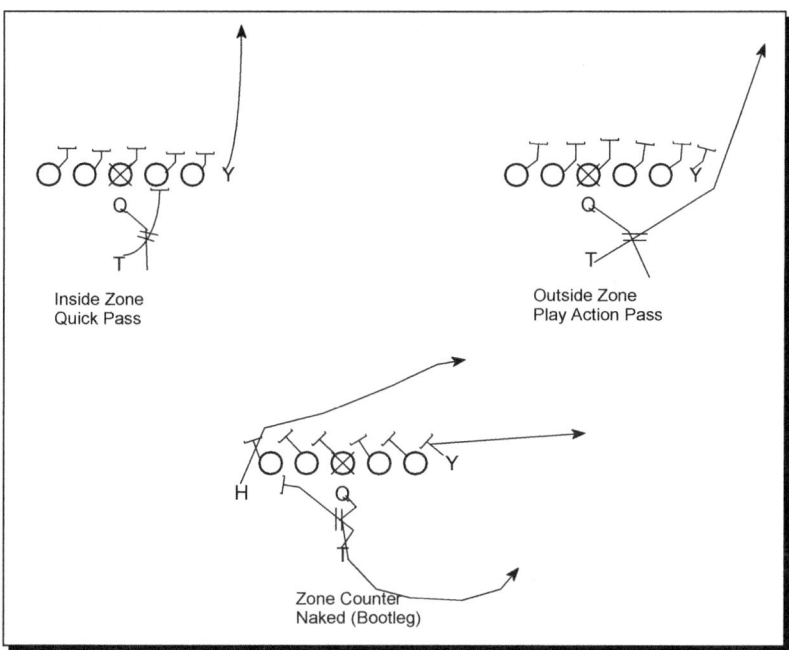

Diagram 4-2. Three complementary zone play-action passes

Could a one-back run offense utilize a one-back power play tied into a quick-pass game check-with-me to help insure that the one-back power isn't running into a seven-man front? Of course, it can. How about a split end-side speed option play, when there is only one defender aligned outside of the weakside offensive tackle? Once again, of course you can. That's all a part of packaging run plays. Furthermore, don't forget running naked (bootleg) play-action passes, quick passes, play-action passes and deeper, more delayed-timing play-action passes to throw to deeper pass routes.

Packages can also be mixed to create an offense. A two-back set with a weak aligned fullback can easily run a weakside zone lead run zone play, with lead isolation packaged with zone counter run play-action strong, as detailed in Diagram 4-3.

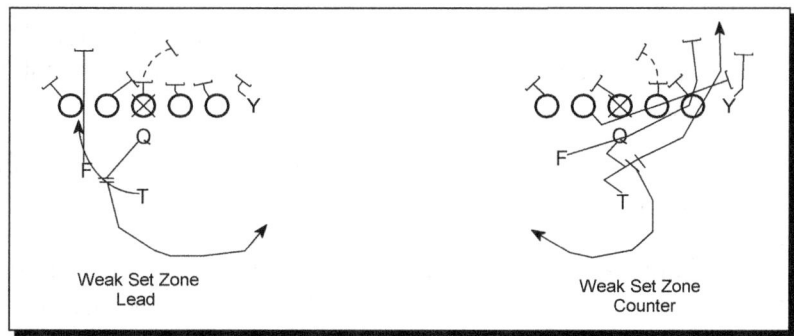

Diagram 4-3. Two packaged weak-set aligned zone run plays

Diagram 4-4 shows three packaged run plays from a strongly aligned fullback. The first run play is a strongside zone lead run play, with lead, isolation block action. The second run play is a strongside outside zone run play, with a lead fullback blocker in the strong safety alley. The third run play is a counter run play to the weakside.

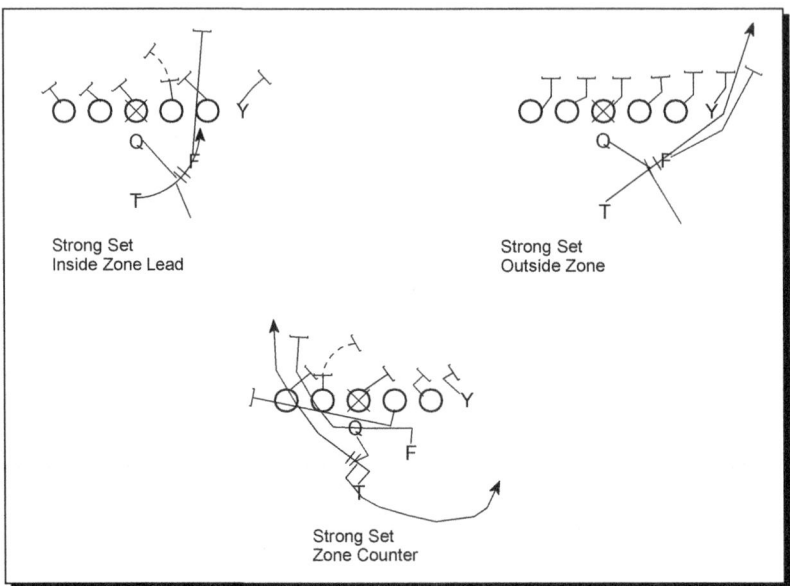

Diagram 4-4. Three packaged strong-set aligned zone run plays

Study and Analyze the Offensive Packages

As has already been addressed, a variety of run and pass play packages can be married into one package to create a total run and pass offense. At this point, another key consideration in putting together a well-balanced, effective offense is to constantly review what you are trying to accomplish in the application of your offense. The key in this instance is to constantly evaluate what you are doing. What seems to be working well? What seems to not be working well? If something is not going well, why keep it? On the other hand, do certain plays still seem to be important, even if they are not working that well? If that's the case, then look to tweak such plays to see if you can find ways to help make such plays better and, as a result, more successful.

The off-season is an excellent time to do a fine-tooth-and-comb analysis of your offense. Such an analysis allows you to thoroughly examine your offense in general on par downs and more specifically on down-and-distance situations, such as third-down offense, red zone offense and two-minute offense. Such specific evaluations can help a coordinator to see that certain plays might be highly successful on par down situations, while being only marginally effective or, even, hardly effective at all, for a number of those down-and-distance situations.

CHAPTER 5
CREATING THE OFFENSE

Chapter 4 reviewed what you need to do, as an offensive staff, with regard to deciding and developing the type of offense you want to use. The pluses and minuses of an offense (the spread passing offense served as an example) were analyzed to point out the importance of working together as a group of offensive coaches. Information was shared and analyzed concerning the type of offense you want in your efforts to come to a decision and finalize the offensive action your team will ultimately utilize. Chapter 5 provides an overview of several of the key factors involved in enabling you to take the next step and put together the type of offense you believe can be successful for your football program.

An Offensive Coordinator Needs to Respect His Gut Feelings

Whenever I've experienced that I had to make a tough, football coaching decision, I found that I knew the answer well before I thought I would. Why did I feel that way? I felt that way because I had long ago learned that after careful analyzation and focused work of culling the information at hand, the answer would, often, become crystal clear.

As a result, I found that continuing the analyzation and the culling of important information only furthered strengthened my belief in the answer at which I ultimately arrived. I came to believe that this scenario was, simply, a process of my mind having the ability to realize the correct answer from the enlightening information our staff had researched and studied. More simply, analyzing and studying the pertinent information at hand produced a gut feeling that rarely was wrong for me. Furthermore, even when I was not totally correct, I found that I wasn't far away from making sound decisions. While that may sound superficial, I've come to realize, however, from my many years of coaching, that if you do your homework diligently, the correct answer is, almost always, not that far away. Such thinking can, and should be, a big part of your decision as to what type of offensive design you should use and to which you should make a commitment.

Strictly Designed Offenses

A well-structured, strictly designed offense such as a wishbone, a wing-T, or an I offense can help to promote extremely disciplined offensive play for a team. A strictly designed offense with regard to personnel and formation usage, coupled with tightly packaged run and pass plays, can greatly help to systemize a total offensive design. As such, utilizing such systemization can make it easier to understand how a defense may try to stop the offense's attack design. The offensive coordinator should be able to quickly see why a segment of his offense, or even a major part of his offense, is being shut down. If the design of the offense is well-structured and thoroughly understood, the offensive coordinator playcaller should be able to make adjustments quickly and efficiently to counter whatever a defense is doing in its effort to stymie the effectiveness of the offense it is encountering.

A strictly and tightly designed offense allows the offensive players to get a tremendous amount of practice repetition. Practicing a more limited amount of technique skills for a more limited amount of run and pass-actions enables the players to get a consistent amount of quality practice work over and over again. For example, the wishbone offense, based on its inside, triple-option threat design, allows for the practice of the triple-option run play design, with a relatively high number of repetitions.

The same factor is true for teams that use run/pass/option (RPO) concepts as a base part of their offenses. A strictly and tightly designed offense is, most often, based on sound run, pass, or run/pass play designs, including supporting, supplemental run and pass plays that augment the base runs and passes. Such plays enhance the base offensive design to help offenses to be complete in their efforts to attack a defense horizontally and/or vertically.

On the other hand, a tight, condensed, offensive structure can also place the offense at a disadvantage, from the standpoint of executing the same, limited run and pass plays over and over. Such a limited amount of total defense can make it easier for a defense to read the flow of an offense, as the offense attempts to execute its offensive run and pass play designs. Defensive recognition is an important part of total defensive execution. Not having enough offensive run, pass, and formation variation threats can definitely help a defense, as it attempts to stop the efforts of a tightly, condensed, offensive structure.

Strictly Designed Offenses Seem to Work Best in High Schools

Tight, strictly designed offenses, for the most part, seem to work best on the high school level. Why? Because high school football programs have far less time to prepare, design, teach, and coach. Furthermore, some high school coaches may have up to five full-time academic courses to teach each and every day. As such, assistant coaches, and even some head high school coaches, may find themselves racing from other schools where they teach to just get to practice on time. The same factor can be true for other members of the coaching staff who may work full-time jobs outside of education during the mornings and early afternoons.

Accordingly, tight, strictly designed offenses may change only slightly from year-to-year. This situation can help to create a level of consistency that coaches and players alike can fall back on due to the inability to have enough overall time to attempt a more complex, overall, time-consuming offensive design and structure.

Using a Tightly Designed Multiple Offense

A number of multiple offensive teams use small, tight packages of runs, passes, and play-action passes that are, or can be, disguised with personnel, formations, shifts, and motion variations to help create multiplicity. In this manner, the runs and passes are, as in strictly designed offenses, kept to a limit to help to provide a greater amount of practice time per run or pass play.

Another possible approach is to utilize multiple runs and pass plays, along with a variety of personnel plans, formations, shifts, and motions, all with the guise of creating difficulties for the opposing defenses. Such multiplicity, whether from run or pass variations or from personnel, formation, shift, and motion variation usage, can be an extremely effective way to keep a defense guessing, as it attempts to stop the offensive attack.

CHAPTER 6
WHAT YOU DO IS IMPORTANT; HOW YOU DO WHAT YOU DO IS MORE IMPORTANT!

The title of this chapter represents an extremely important concept with regard to the type of offense a coordinator may choose to utilize. What you do is important. Having a balanced, well-designed offense, which efficiently attacks a defense horizontally from sideline to sideline with both its pass and run game, is key. A balanced, well-designed offense also efficiently assaults a defense vertically from the line of scrimmage to the opponent's end zone with both its pass and run game. As such, a balanced, efficient, well-designed offense is well-packaged so that the run, option, dropback pass, and play-action pass plays support and feed off of one another to help produce an offense that is consistently hard for defenses to stop, no matter how good those defenses might otherwise be.

Too Much Offense?

On occasion, however, what you do may often be too much for your players and your coaches to handle. That's the underlying basis of the statement "… how you do what you do is more important!" Quite simply, the more you do, the more your players have to learn and master. Similarly, the more you do offensively, the more your coaches will have to teach and coach. Furthermore, the more total offense you have, the less the amount of practice repetitions per play that your players will have to get ready for their game time preparation.

Some coaches are often heard complaining about the lack of production from their "... sophisticated ..." offense. When I observe such offenses, the first factor that comes to my mind is that the team's offense has too much total offense. As a result, the team's offensive players and, probably, its coaches are being asked to do too much.

Yes, your offense needs balance and a sound run and pass game. On the other hand, however, too much is, simply ... too much! What can be worse is for a team to have an overly diverse, all-star type offense utilizing most every key run or pass play known to mankind.

Such offenses have no concern for balance or the use of key supplemental run and pass plays that are very essential in helping to make those key run and pass plays go. For example, the outside zone run play supplements the inside zone run play. The zone counter play helps to supplement both the base inside and outside zone counter plays. Naked bootleg action off the inside and outside zone plays helps to give further, valuable, misdirection balance to the total package of the offense. Furthermore, play-action passes for the base inside and outside zone run plays further help to enhance the total effectiveness of the entire zone offensive package, given that the play-action passes are able to strike up the field to stretch defenses deep, as well as attack both zone and man-to-man coverages.

Zone offenses have progressed into shotgun, read-option action offenses—read-give action, with a running back; read-keep action by the quarterback, and possible read-triple option action to trailing pitch backs to help create devastating double and triple option give/keep/pitch packages. In fact, if quick pass game run/pass options (RPOs) are added, an offense can have an attack design that can be very difficult for a defense to stop.

The use of specifically designed play-action passes to supplement a run game helps to give a coordinator a well-designed, well-packaged offense. Not only does it allow for a tight, completely balanced offense, it is also not too much for the players to execute and for the coaches to teach and coach. Still, the key in this instance is to realize that while what a coordinator and his offense does is, certainly, important, how coaches and his players do in relation to what is being done is far more important.

K.I.S.S. (Keep It Simple, Stupid)

"Keep it simple, Stupid" is a saying that has been around the world of sports for a long, long time. Football is, certainly, no exception. As I already have alluded to, the word "... sophistication ..." is often not necessarily a good term to utilize when putting together an offense. An offensive coordinator should not make the mistake of thinking that sophistication within an offense is necessarily a good thing, if such sophistication results in difficulty ... complexity ... or even outright confusion. Actually, the simpler the execution requires when it comes to the fundamentals of the game of football, the greater the chance of quality execution.

An offense often has enough problems to contend with when trying to run block an overpowering defensive lineman or pass protect a quarterback versus an all-out blitz. Trying to execute sophisticated, difficult-to-execute blocking schemes can be yet another possible unduly challenging obstacle. It's important to make sure that you, the offensive coordinator, are not the reason that your offense is having execution difficulties. As such, cleanly executed blocking schemes with simple blocking assignments greatly help to negate difficult to handle defensive stunts and blitzes. The same factor is true for the execution of an offense's pass patterns, run-option plays, or a quarterback's pass progression reads. Keep it simple, Stupid!

If in Doubt, Cut Back

If a coordinator feels he has too much offense on his plate for him, his coaches, and his players, then the chances are that he does. If so, he needs to cut back. One of his initial steps should be to analyze his offense. What is working well? What is not working well? First of all, he should eliminate what has not been working well, unless he absolutely feels that it is important to have certain plays in his offense, as well as in his game plan. What plays does he have on his ready-list arsenal that he doesn't seem to use come game time? As such, he should get rid of those plays or put them on hold for, possibly, a specific game opponent.

Fix What Needs Fixing ... Now!

In Chapter 4, a definite emphasis on a coordinator and his staff constantly evaluating and analyzing the progress of an offense both during a season and at the end of a season was addressed. In reality, a statistical analysis should be made after each and every game played, and the single-game analysis of the most previous game should be tacked onto an already ongoing seasonal analysis. In this fashion, a team's ongoing yearly analysis can be instantly investigated by simply pushing the appropriate keys on the computer.

Early in the season is a good time for dropping run or pass plays that don't seem to be helping the total, positive, offensive output. Whether they are too tough, too complex to execute, or seem to not fit into the total offensive scheme and design, the coordinator must be able to understand that dropping such plays from the total package can be a proactive, positive step in slimming or trimming of the total offense. Such actions alleviate unnecessary, unwanted weight on the offensive package. It is important to note, however, that it may take as much as a half-season to realize that a specific play is a drag on the total offense—be it a run or a pass. One way or the other, the first step a coordinator should take, in this regard, is to see if a run or pass play that is being scrutinized can be fixed so that it can become an integral part of the offense.

Fixing means giving a focused effort in the offensive staff room and on the practice field to remedy whatever is wrong with a run or pass play that is being looked at with regard to being kept in the playbook or not. First of all, the coordinator and offensive coaches must thoroughly analyze if the play in question is worth saving. Does it fit the rest of the offense? Does it add to the offense's total design, and to its effectiveness? Is it a poor play for the offense, because of its execution difficulties or because the players required to execute the fundamentals of the play are not good enough to do so? To keep such a play, the coordinator must be willing to put extra planning and practice time into fixing what the offensive staff ascertains needs fixing. If the coordinator doesn't feel he can make such a commitment, he should move on to fix other parts of his offense.

"W-I-N"—What's Important Now!

I have long been a fan from afar of Coach Lou Holtz through his storied football coaching career. One of my favorite quotes from Coach Holtz is "W-I-N, WHAT'S IMPORTANT NOW!" The "W-I-N" acronym of "…what's important now!" states, simply, that it is important to focus … to concentrate on what is important now … right now! In other words, examine … find out what is wrong and then immediately fix it. Don't wait!

The "W-I-N" concept is an extremely important concept for any aspect of a football program, including recruiting, academic considerations, conditioning, special teams, defense, and offense. It's important for the head coach, the coordinators, and the position coaches.

In that regard, it's important for the offensive coordinator to thoroughly examine each and every portion of his offensive program and then to determine "… what's important now." As noted previously, he should, then, do whatever is necessary to fix what needs fixing.

Far too often, coaches will push a problem to the side in an effort to hope the problem will go away by itself. In reality, it will almost never go away by itself. For example, if you feel you need to suddenly utilize your rarely used trap scheme to trap and kick-out a hard rushing defensive lineman as part of a specific game plan, then you must focus on providing the necessary teaching, coaching, and practice time needed to help make that trap play successful. Determine "… what's important now … keep it simple, Stupid … cut back if necessary and … fix what needs fixing!"

Sweat the Small Stuff

Often, coaches worry about the big stuff, when it's the little stuff that bites you on the ankle and ends up causing big problems. I firmly believe that the best way to take care of the big stuff is to take care of the small stuff first and foremost.

During my career, I was taught by my head coach at the time, Homer Smith, an excellent teaching, coaching, and practice system for the center/quarterback exchange. At first, Coach Smith's system seemed quite different to me. Quickly, however, I found out how right Coach Smith was. Putting the football on the ground due to improper center/quarterback exchange techniques was just not going to happen at West Point, and it didn't.

Frankly, I can't remember the actual streak number of successful center/quarterback exchange snaps in the three years I coached at Army. I do remember that the streak of successful snaps and snap receptions reached long into those three seasons. I can also remember Homer lying on the ground in front of one of our centers looking up to see the actual snap exchange action. He wanted to be sure that the football was properly being wedged in between the heels of the quarterback's hands.

At West Point, with our limited amount or practice time minutes, a pre-practice, five-minute period officially started the daily practices. The special, pre-practice, five-minute drill period was set for the offense to have the centers and quarterbacks practice their center/quarterback exchanges. Forty years later, I'm still coaching that five minute, pre-practice, center/quarterback exchange drill. The only change is that now my teams finish their daily practices with a second, five-minute post-practice period to practice the center/quarterback for a second time of the practice. This schedule is an example of the fact that stressing the small things can produce positive results.

CHAPTER 7
THE OFFENSIVE COORDINATOR AS THE LEADER OF THE OFFENSE

The offensive coordinator is, normally, the leader of the offense. In reality, the offensive coordinator acts as the head coach of the offense or close to it. As was discussed in Chapter 1, the offensive coordinator's role may have full authority to make the decisions and utilize his skill set to produce the specific offensive design he believes will help the offense to be successful. Then again, in some scenarios, the coordinator might work closely with the head coach to enable the two to create an effective offense together.

On the other hand, the offensive coordinator might not be the true leader of the offense at all. It might, very well, be the offensive coordinator's role to specifically be the manager of the efforts of the offense in the offense's efforts to be successful, with leadership mostly coming from the head coach. In this chapter, the focus is on the offensive coordinator who acts as the head coach of the offense—the true leader of the offense, first and foremost. The bottom line is in order to have a successful football program, there must be strong leadership.

The offensive coordinator should be the visionary of the offense. He is the person who should know what type of offense he desires to utilize in the team's efforts to score points and be effective in all facets of offensive play. As a result, it is the offensive coordinator who should know what type of offense can best help the football program be successful. Once he establishes the parameters of his team's offensive design, he must be responsible for setting realistic and challenging goals for both the offensive staff and the offensive players. Furthermore, he must work diligently to develop a well-designed offense that attacks both the strengths and weaknesses of opposing defenses.

The offensive coordinator must have the flexibility to adjust to the many demanding, often taxing, game-like situations that so frequently arise during the course of a game and during the course of a season that can so easily lead to a sidetracked, underperforming offense. To take this one step forward, the offensive coordinator must also be able to effectively fight adversity, with a tenacious, rally-the-troops mentality, when his offensive players' backs are to the wall. He must be able to exhibit solid drive, rigid determination, sound initiative, noticeable energy, earnest motivation, and a rock-solid commitment to do all he can possibly do as the leader of the offense.

An offensive coordinator must display a sound character at all times. Such character must entail integrity, sound ethics, and trust in his relationship with both his assistant coaches and his players. The offensive coordinator should be an honorable person, an individual who is unselfish, who cares about the well-being of others, and who is willing to accept responsibility for himself, as well as for the people under his charge. Such an offensive coordinator must have a sincere desire to help develop playing skills and personal attributes as players, students, and citizens of their home town, home state, and country.

Leaders Are Made Much More Than Being Inherent

I strongly believe that most leaders are made, not born, with great leadership skills. Certain skills, such as leadership, often seem to be far from the world of football and sports in general. Truth be known, most great leaders are not born with great leadership skills. Not only are they taught, they have learned leadership through both study and their personal life experiences.

When I was appointed to my first, college-level, offensive coordinator's job, I was immensely fortunate to have been sent to the Dale Carnegie program by Larry Smith, the head coach at the University of Arizona. At first, I was a bit miffed about why I had to attend classes concerning people skills, public speaking, management, and leadership. I soon realized that to that point in my career, while I had developed a sound background of football teaching and coaching skills, I had much to learn.

As I participated in the Dale Carnegie program, I quickly found out that there was a whole, new world of knowledge I needed to know if I was to become a successful football offensive coordinator and head coach. To become an efficient football offensive coordinator, all of the pieces to the puzzle must be connected. The study of leadership and the soon-to-be-addressed topic of management are key aspects to becoming a successful football offensive coordinator.

Taking Dale Carnegie leadership and management-type courses are not required, especially when someone can purchase books on leadership and management, often very inexpensively. In addition, of course, the Internet has also opened a whole, new resource world of knowledge concerning leadership and management, as well as other invaluable topics, that collectively can help enable an offensive coordinator to become all he is capable of being. Whether leading the assistant coaches or the offensive players on the team, the offensive coordinator must lead the charge in the offense's efforts to help the team win! Furthermore, when he leads that charge, he must do it in as professional manner as possible.

CHAPTER 8
THE OFFENSIVE COORDINATOR AS THE MANAGER OF THE OFFENSE

This chapter deals with the term "management," specifically management skills for the offensive coordinator. In this regard, leadership is the act of enlisting staff and players to support efforts to help accomplish set, common, offensive football goals. Management is the organization and coordination of those efforts to achieve those particular goals. Together, strong leadership and strong management can greatly help to produce successful offensive football play.

Football is a complex game played by 22 players at a time, with 11 players from each opposing team facing off against one another. That's a lot of player personnel on the field at one time. On top of that, you then have to add the specialization of the game, the various types of offenses and defenses and their play, as well as the large variety of distinct special team's play.

On offense, alone, you have to be concerned with par down offense (first and second down), third-down offense, red zone offense, goal line offense, two-minute offense, desperation offense, slowdown offense, kill-the-clock offense and coming-out offense. As such, that's a tremendous amount of isolated, separated, offensive football play during the course of a game.

The aforementioned certainly entails a significant level of management—to be sure that all facets of offensive play are well-planned, organized, coordinated, and practiced. The practice elements, whether classroom chalk talks, pre- or post-practice walk-through drills, warm-up/stretch/run drills, individual drills, unit/combination drills, 7-on-7 pass drills, full team drills, or post-practice conditioning drills, must all be thoroughly and carefully managed via planning, organization, and coordination for each, and every, moment of a practice.

For the offensive coordinator, this factor means having to wait for the overall practice plan from the head coach so that the offensive coordinator can then plan the overall offensive practice plan in the periods of the practice left vacant by the head coach. As a rule, the offensive coordinator will then leave certain blocks of time for the individual position coaches to plan their individual drills.

Offensive Game Situation Experts

At this point of the practice planning, the offensive coordinator can fill in all of the open practice periods left vacant by the head coach, including the actual practice scripts, with the offensive plays and defensive scout alignments. Depending on the circumstances, the coordinator may have the time during the school day to fill out every period that needs scripting, even if that work is extensive.

Another way to fill out the practice scripts is to use offensive game plan situational experts. This approach involves a concept that can be very helpful in actually creating game-situation experts, in an effort to share the load of an entire game plan attack. For example, the tight end coach can be the goal line expert. In the planning of the actual, ready-list game plan, he would be the coach to break down all of the video of the opposing team's goal line defense. He would then draw up a preliminary goal line game plan to be presented to the entire offensive staff for their evaluation of the goal line expert's suggestions. With the offensive coordinator having the final say so, a final goal line ready list would then be put together.

Subsequently, suggestions might be made by the staff with regard to the goal line expert's preliminary thoughts. Perhaps, a different goal line play that the goal line expert hadn't thought of might then be added. In addition, adding a motion or a shift or running a suggested pass play from a different formational look might be a better alternative than what was originally proposed.

Such a system breaks down the total number of the game plan and practice-script action with which a singular assistant coach or the offensive coordinator might have to contend. In addition, the "expert" concept helps to create accomplished game-plan coaches, who truly become experts in their specific, assigned situational. As such, this process helps the game-plan expert to focus on one or two game-plan concepts each game week. Furthermore, this "expert" system helps to train young, less-experienced assistant coaches in their assigned expert roles, as more and more is assigned to them either once they start to grasp what the coordinator is looking for or as they come up with an excellent game-plan suggestion of their own.

In such a system, the offensive coordinator is still the boss. (Of course, the head coach is the boss of the offensive coordinator.) On the other hand, as time goes on, it is amazing at how quickly such inexperienced coaches will catch on, as they learn more and more with regard to offensive play and game-plan concepts. When a totally new assistant coach joins the staff, it then becomes the role of the coordinator or another experienced veteran coach to help bring such a new coach up to snuff in this area.

The underlying thought process for an offensive coordinator is to plan, organize, and then coordinate to help an offense meet its set goals on a weekly and seasonal basis. Once this objective is accomplished, as a result of strong leadership and strong management, the offense will find itself in a definitive position to help the team succeed.

Management Delegation

To be able to utilize a system, such as offensive game-plan situational experts, the offensive coordinator must be willing to delegate specific workloads to his assistant coaches. In reality, he needs to do that whether he employs the situational game-plan expert's concept or not. Many coordinators try to "… do it all …" when it comes to the offense's organizational workload. Unfortunately, more often than not, that's not always the best way to do it.

In all likelihood, a new offensive coordinator will quickly see that he has some very capable, veteran coaches on his staff. If that's not the case, he will want to be sure to hire such capable, veteran coaches or even young coaches who seem to display near-veteran capabilities. The offensive coordinator should delegate key workload concepts to the assistant coaches that he has deemed as being adept and proficient. Doing so allows the offensive coordinator to work with the coaches he may inherit or hire, who may not, as of yet, be as adept or proficient as he would like them to be. This situation helps to create a balance on the offensive staff, with the offensive coordinator being able to rely on the coaching abilities of his veteran assistant coaches, as he works to develop the skills of younger, less-informed and less-experienced coaches at this particular point in their careers.

As was previously noted, the offensive coordinator cannot do everything of importance with regard to the offense by himself, thus the need for delegation. With such delegation comes the responsibility of the individual offensive staff members to perform their assignments to the best of their abilities. As such, it is extremely important for the offensive coordinator to hold his assistant coaches accountable for their assigned, delegated workloads.

If, for any reason, the delegated workload is not sufficiently undertaken to appropriate standards/expectations, the resulting situation then falls back into the lap of the offensive coordinator. The offensive coordinator, or another veteran assistant coach on the staff, is the person needed, at this point, to assist the faltering coach. All in all, such assistance is virtually indispensable, so that that particular coach can sufficiently learn how to meet the goals of what is expected of him. As has already been stated, the offensive coordinator and his staff must evaluate, evaluate, and then evaluate some more, on a daily, weekly, and seasonal basis, to be sure that all necessary offensive teaching and coaching concepts are being properly addressed.

CHAPTER 9
THE ALL-IMPORTANT YEARLY PLANNING

A number of coaches will clean out their lockers, pack up their bags, and stow away their gear the day after the last game of the football season. The only major concern is the planning of the soon-to-be, after-season awards banquet. Other than that, it's often "… wait for next year!" Of course, on the high school level and even on some of the lower-level Division II and Division III programs, many coaches will find themselves coaching a second or third sport as an assistant or even as a head coach. On the other hand, head coaches and coordinators can often find the off-season to be an extremely efficient and effective way to analyze, study, and plan for the next upcoming football season.

First of all, I don't agree with the train of thought that once the football season is over, it's truly over. In high schools and colleges, the football season has become a year-round endeavor, rightly or wrongly. More often than not, the winter season starts out as an extremely busy time of the year, with all of the holiday celebrations.

December, however, also becomes the start of college football bowl season, culminating in the annual college football playoff championship series. About that same time, the NFL starts the season-ending battles for the final playoff slots and the actual playoff games, in an effort by teams to get to the Super Bowl. For most football coaches, this has always been a fun time of the year, with all of the holiday activities and for all of the great bowl games and playoff games to watch.

The advent of being able to easily record such bowl and playoff games on television has given an offensive coordinator the ability to watch, analyze, and study many of the top college bowl and playoff teams, as well as the NFL playoff teams. In reality, with overlapping times for all of these games, it's virtually impossible to watch and study all of the bowl and playoff games. On the other hand, as the offensive coordinator, I can pick and choose what I feel could be the most beneficial games for me to analyze and study.

During the college bowl and pro playoff season, I ALWAYS have a notepad next to me, as I watch the games and listen to the commentary. Furthermore, of course, television playback abilities can allow me to go over and over specific plays, just as I might watch videotapes in our staff room. I am careful to watch key games, whose offenses I wanted to study that were similar to ours. In addition, I ask my staff to watch, take notes, and report on one or two (or three or four) of such bowl or playoff games. In that regard, I ask them to jot down any good ideas with regard to plays or techniques they saw in such games, whether I assigned them specific games to watch or not.

Over the years, I really enjoyed when we decided on study dates on the calendar to get together and report on the "good" ideas the coaches have discovered. As much as I asked for potential ideas to analyze and consider, I also wanted my coaches and myself to be cognizant with regard to what type pf plays hurt certain types of defenses, whether it was the total structure of the defenses, runs, coverages, stunts, or blitzes. From a coordinator's standpoint, I always have liked studying patterns of what type of runs and passes hurt the types of defenses we would see of the schools on our schedule for the next season.

Attending Clinics

Attending clinics after the first of the calendar year often seems to truly put the new football season in motion. It might be the colossal American Football Coaches Association Convention or one of the various state, regional, or local clinics. One way or the other, the offensive coordinator should be cognizant of the possible clinics he, as well as his staff, could possibly attend.

In reality, finances are often a consideration for each attendee, especially if airfare and lodging are considerations. When deciding whether or not to attend a particular clinic, the speaking topics should be carefully examined in advance to determine what the desires are for specific attendance and presentations. Furthermore, a local county, league, or conference clinic may be worth attending, no matter whether the clinic is highly considered for its presentation talks or not, especially from a networking standpoint. The American Football Coaches Association Clinic itself helps to create a tremendous job-networking clinic, which facilitates making new friends and colleagues and catching up with old acquaintances.

I like to work the "… delegation …" (that word once again), when attending clinics. If there are two clinic talks being made at the same time to which I would like to listen, I assign one or two assistant coaches to one of the clinic talks that I, personally, won't be able to attend. Furthermore, I make sure that my assistant coaches, who attended talks other than the ones I participated in, carefully take notes to be shared with the rest of the staff, once the clinic is over. Networking is certainly an important part of going to clinics. On the other hand, I want to be sure that my assistant coaches are attending and taking notes on the presentations the staff is interested in hearing about, analyzing, and studying.

Visiting Other Football Programs

During the spring season, visiting college football programs is an excellent learning resource for a coordinator and his staff. Of course, travel and hotel costs could be prohibitive. On the other hand, since some junior colleges and four-year college programs are located in-state, an offensive coordinator and his staff would have relatively little difficulty in visiting them. Frankly, it is counterproductive and a waste of a good learning opportunity for a local resource to be ignored. As a rule, most junior colleges, Division II, and Division III level programs would feel honored to share knowledge with an offensive coordinator's program and, in the process, they would do a good job of doing so.

It is also a good idea to consider visiting high school programs, especially if they employ an offense similar, or somewhat similar, to your offense. In reality, there are numerous high school coaches who are more than excited about the possibility of sharing ideas with fellow high schools. Of course, it's probably inappropriate to share information with a team from your own league or conference. On the other hand, there are many programs, not in your league, that are willing and able to visit with you and your staff.

Using Ready Lists

As such, a ready list is an inventory of all of the runs and passes that were employed during the past season. The initial ready list for the new year and new season should actually be an accumulation of all of the ready lists from the previous season's games put together in one, large, season-ending inventory. In reality, starting with the previous season's accumulated ready list provides the offensive coordinator with a base from which to begin, as he and his staff analyze and study in an effort to determine which run and pass plays they want to keep and which ones they may want to eliminate.

The accumulated, end-of-the-year ready list becomes the true starting point for the new, upcoming season. Pulling out the previous, end-of-the-year ready lists allows the coordinator a chance to thoroughly examine and evaluate the ready list of plays from the previous season to see which run or pass plays should be kept and which ones should, or could, be eliminated. Such an analysis can, possibly, make the coordinator realize that he may need some new offensive thinking for the new, upcoming season.

On the other hand, upon studying the ready list, the offensive coordinator might realize that he is on the right track and only needs to do a bit of tweaking to fine-tune the offense as it is.

Football Classes

With the growth of year-round football, or close to it, physical education football classes have become quite common during the spring semester of the school year. Such classes are usually non-padded, non-contact classes, with no football gear other than footballs and, possibly, helmets or helmet liners for safety. The focal points for these classes tend to be stretching, conditioning, agility work, weight lifting, and skills development. Some football class programs will utilize "… walk-through …" type teaching drills. For the most part, the classes deal with conditioning and skill drills that involve no contact.

Planning for such physical education football class practices is typically accomplished in time-block forms for a 50-minute class (or, for whatever amount of time such a class is allotted). For example, a coach may choose to have five, 10-minute blocks of teaching and coaching time to practice basic football agility or skill drills. For easier organization, the class could be organized into five, separate groups that are rotated every 10 minutes, employing a variety of such drills each day. If there is enough room, since many of such classes might have to be undertaken in small, indoor facilities, there could be two separate rotations of football drill actions, one for the offense and one for the defense.

Coaches may prefer to have blocks of time during football classes for the teaching and coaching of large-group skills, such as seven-on-seven pass drills, pitting offensive and defensive personnel. Play script-type planning would be used for such seven-on-seven pass drills or for any other team-type drills that the offensive coordinator might want to coach and practice.

What is most important in this situation is that the offensive coordinator must be sure the drill work is done in well-planned, time blocks that can allow for a maximum amount of football skill practice in relatively short periods of the normal school-day class periods. In addition, the coordinator must be sure that he has a plan for possible harsh winter and spring class practice days.

Spring Practice

Spring practice is common to almost all levels of play on the college level. In high school, however, there are still many states that do not allow for spring practices. In reality, the number of states that don't permit high school spring practices has been rapidly decreasing.

Spring practices come in all shapes and forms. Some states allow for 10 to 15 practices, some as much as 20 or more. Some states allow for only non-padded spring practices, while others are conducted in full gear. Helmet liners are often used if helmets are not allowed for spring practice. One way or another, a football program and its offensive coordinator must follow the set guidelines established by governing state, regional, local, conference, or league regulations.

Spring practice must, initially, contend with the graduation of the previous senior class. As a result, underclass players from the prior season are asked to step up to fill in starting player roles, as well as meet the need for new, key backup roles. At this point, it is important for the offensive coordinator and his staff to analyze and determine who the new starters and key backup players will be by the end of the spring practices. On the other hand, the coordinator and his staff must also be sure to be sufficiently flexible come the beginning of fall, pre-season practice sessions, figuring that at least a few of the backup players will mature over the summer, enabling them to challenge for starting roles.

Spring practice should be looked at as the true, on-the-field start of the new season at hand, if spring practice is allowed. The base plays of a team's offense (culled from the previous season's ready list) should be the starting point for the offense, with an allowance for possible new run and/or pass plays. If the coordinator has decided to add some new plays, those plays should be put to use early in spring practice, so that there is plenty of time to enable the coordinator to properly evaluate if he wants to keep the new plays or not. Spring practice is also a good time for experimentation, be it in the run or pass games. In addition, spring practices offer an excellent opportunity to focus on individual player fundamental development.

Setting a Practice Calendar

The first thing a coordinator should do for spring practice (if spring practice is allowed) and pre-season practices is to set a practice calendar for the utilized periods of time. Using a monthly calendar format helps to detail when and, possibly, where all practices and scrimmages will be. In addition, such a pre-season calendar schedule helps inform all coaches, players, administrators, and parents of important dates and times. Diagram 9-1 details a pre-season calendar, spanning the three-week period (16 practice days) prior to the first game week of the season.

Sunday	Monday	Tuesday	Wednesday	Thursday	Friday	Saturday
30	31	1	2	3	4	5
6	7	8	9	10	11	12
13	14 Helmets only Practice #1 2:45 p.m.	15 Helmets only Practice #2 2:45 p.m.	16 Helmets only Practice #3 2:45 p.m.	17 Helmets and shoulder pads Practice #4 2:45 p.m.	18 Helmets and shoulder pads Practice #5 2:45 p.m.	19 Helmets and shoulder pads Practice #6 10 a.m. Guest speaker
20	21 Full gear Practice #7 2:45 p.m.	22 Helmets and shoulder pads Practice #8 2:45 p.m.	23 Full gear Practice #9 2:45 p.m.	24 Helmets and shoulder pads Practice #10 2:45 p.m.	25 Helmets only Practice #11 2:45 p.m.	26 Full gear Practice #12 (Red and Blue scrimmage) 9 a.m. Booster barbecue
27	28 Full gear Practice #13 2:45 p.m.	29 Full gear Practice #14 2:45 p.m.	30 Helmets and shoulder pads Practice #15 2:45 p.m.	31 Helmets only Practice #16 2:45 p.m.	1 Game #1 7 p.m. Home	2

Diagram 9-1. Model pre-season practice calendar

Note that each calendar-type square includes the date of the day and a sequential number and date for each practice. Furthermore, it also designates the dress for the day, whether it was just helmets, helmets and shoulder pads, or full gear. In addition, all support functions should be carefully listed to help all players and coaches be sure that they are informed about miscellaneous outings, including when and where they should be for such functions.

CHAPTER 10
DAILY PRACTICE PLANNING

Daily practice plans can, actually, be the best way to help lay out a total spring ball practice plan, and an overall pre-season practice plan, as well as in-season weekly practice plans. Offensive coordinators can formulate any type of daily practice plan they want. In reality, a number of coaches are taught to utilize 24, five-minute period daily practice periods to allow for the greatest amount of daily practice plan flexibility. The five-minute practice period set-ups provide the coordinator with the opportunity for flexible, short period practice segments, as shown in Diagram 10-1.

Date _____			Gear _____		
Period	**RB**	**QB**	**WR**	**TE**	**O-Line**
1					
2					
3					
4					
5					
6					
7					
8					
9					
10					
11					
12					
13					
14					
15					
16					
17					
18					
19					
20					
21					
22					
23					
24					

Diagram 10-1. Daily 24, five-minute, practice plan blocks

Short, five-minute practice segments can easily be tied together to allow 10-minute, 15-minute or more practice time blocks. Diagram 10-2 shows how five-minute practice blocks can be tied together for longer unit and team time block practice periods. In this instance, a unit time block refers to practice work that is not individual nor is it full team practice work. For example, two examples of unit-type drills would be the offensive line, working on a pass, blitz pick-up drill, while the quarterback, running backs, wide receivers, and tight ends focus on executing specific pass route patterns.

Date _____ **Gear**_____ **Full**_____

Period	RB	QB	WR	TE	O-Line
1	Special teams Field goal/extra point	QB pass warm-ups	Special teams Field goal/extra point		Special teams Field goal/extra point protection
2	Special teams Field goal/extra point	QB pass warm-ups	Special teams Field goal/extra point		Special teams Field goal/extra point protection
3	Special teams	Net-target throwing	Kickoff return Punt return		Pass pro block progression
4	Special teams	Net-target throwing	Kickoff return Punt return		Pass pro block progression
5	Individual drills	QB route throws to WRs		Individual drills (blocking)	Run block progression
6	Individual drills	QB route throws to WRs		Individual drills (blocking)	Run block progression
7	QB route throws to RBs and TEs		Individual drills (blocking)	QB route throws to RBs and TEs	Block twists vs. scouts
8	QB route throws to RBs and TEs		Individual drills (blocking)	QB route throws to RBs and TEs	Block twists vs. scouts
9	Mesh drill with WRs			Individual drills (passing)	Pass pro blocking with defense
10	Mesh drill with TEs		JUGS machine catching	Mesh drill with QBs	Pass pro blocking with defense
11	1-on-1 pass vs. defense				Run blocking with defense
12	1-on-1 pass vs. defense				Run blocking with defense
13	Scramble drill				Pulling drills
14	Anti-blitz 7-on-7 pick-up vs. scouts				Blitz pick-up vs. scouts
15	Anti-blitz 7-on-7 pick-up vs. scouts				Blitz pick-up vs. scouts
16	Red zone 7-on-7 pass vs. scouts				Dropback pass blocking techniques
17	Red zone 7-on-7 pass vs. scouts				Dropback pass blocking techniques
18	Red zone 7-on-7 pass vs. scouts				Dropback pass blocking techniques
19	Red zone 7-on-7 pass vs. scouts				Dropback pass blocking techniques
20	Offensive team red zone vs. scouts (thud)				
21	Offensive team red zone vs. scouts (thud)				
22	Offensive team red zone vs. scouts (thud)				
23	Offensive team red zone vs. defense (thud)				
24	Offensive team red zone vs. defense (thud)				

Diagram 10-2. Five-minute practice blocks, being tied together to allow for longer practice blocks of times

Note in Diagram 10-2 that the last six periods of the practice shown in Diagram 10-1 are taken up by six, five-minute periods of an assigned red zone scrimmage drill against the defense. This set-up is another example of the flexible use of a two-hour, 24 five-minute practice block structure.

Pre-Season Practice

Pre-season practice takes on the importance of precise game preparation for the soon-to-arrive first game of the season. On the other hand, there still must be a strong focus on individual fundamental play for all offensive positions. There must also be the interaction of varied unit play, such as the entire offensive line practicing run-trap blocking action or the quarterbacks throwing to tight end and wide receiver routes.

A number of coordinators will plan such pre-season, daily practices on a daily basis. They might, simply, work on a practice plan (or two for two-a-day practices) for the next day's practice. They are able to use this pattern of daily practice plan preparation until the first week of actual game week preparation. Arguably, the best way for the offensive coordinator to prepare his pre-season daily practice plans, with subsequent situational, practice play scripts, is to have all of those practice plans worked on and completed in the summer before the first day of pre-season practice.

By having those pre-season practice plans addressed and completed before the first day of pre-season practice, the offensive coordinator and his staff can be well-prepared to concentrate on coaching, teaching, and staying as fresh as possible for the long haul of the upcoming football season. Furthermore, if any of such practice plans need alterations, the offensive coordinator is in a position to quickly make such additions or deletions.

By pre-planning for the pre-season practices and the careful spacing of the key, critical, situational practice needs, the offensive coordinator is able to insure for such needs as coming-out offense from his own one-yard line, all facets of third- and fourth-down offense, two-minute hurry/hurry offense, trick plays, four-minute slow/slow offense to run out the clock, kill-the-clock offense, red zone offense, and goal line offense. In reality, all of these key, critical game situations can easily be the difference between winning or losing.

In addition, the offensive coordinator is able to prevent any planning log jams of the specific, valuable, practice needs, as the pre-season starts to close in on the team's opening game of the season. A method that has helped me greatly with spring practice (if allowed) and pre-season practice planning is to put empty practice plans (an 8 X 11 blank empty daily practice plan) on a wall or portable white board in a dated and sequentially numbered, monthly calendar fashion.

Each blank practice plan schedule is set up for a maximum of two hours (24, five-minute block segments that can be attached to one another for whatever individual, unit, or team-type drills that are needed for practice). It should be noted that this schedule does not account for such concerns as warm-ups or warm-downs, stretching, or conditioning during the 24, five-minute practice block segments.

The coordinator should understand that in the 15, or so, total pre-season practices, the key critical game situations can be practiced a number of times. On the other hand, while the head coach or offensive coordinator might want to have one, long, major scrimmage for the last, pre-season practice, he might prefer three relatively short, 20- to 30-minute scrimmages, one for red zone offense, one for third-down offense and one for blitz pick-up offense, inserted carefully into the overall, pre-season practices.

Other key critical game situation work might be included for short, two-period, thud (non-tackle) practices. For example, popular seven-on-seven pass drills might take up four to six periods of practice, with a designated emphasis during each practiced seven-on-seven pass drill, such as third-down pass offense, red zone pass offense, and even anti-blitz pass offense. As such, evenly distributing the practice of key critical game situations in small time blocks can have a positive impact on the offense.

CHAPTER 11
GAME WEEK PLANNING

Given the flexibility potential of time usage, when game planning for an actual in-season game is taking place, there are some specific, and often varied, game planning techniques and methods that can be utilized. For example, in that regard, the following tenets have served me well over the course of my years as an offensive coordinator.

Watch Opponent as a Full Staff

An offensive coordinator may not be the person who would dictate the idea of watching the next opponent together as an entire offensive-defensive staff. It is an excellent suggestion, however, to take to the head coach, with the hope that he will buy into the concept. The thought process is to have the entire staff watch the first half of the next opponent's latest game together. If the next opponent played that game against a team that utilized an offbeat offense or defense, then I'd be sure to check out the next most recent game that your opponent has played. If it's the first game of the season, I would then check out the last game of the previous season that your opponent played.

The underlying premise in this situation is to have the entire staff get a feel for what they are up against versus the team they will be playing come game time. At a minimum, for example, such a step will quickly enable the staff to discern how tough a game your team may be in for. A great, pressuring defense? A dominant run-oriented offense, with an excellent play-action game to supplement the run game? Does your offensive staff realize that they're going to have to score a lot of points? Does the defense feel they are going to have to take chances and, perhaps, blitz a lot more or mix up different alignment looks to stop the opponent's potent run game? Is this a game that looks like a potential runaway? In that regard, because you should likely be favored by two touchdowns, should you just focus on sound, basic offensive and defensive play? As such, an approach of having the full staff analyze the fire power potential of the next week's opponent can help to create a realistic and earnest picture of the game-related issues and problems at hand.

As the offensive coordinator, I always loved hearing the words of my head coach when he would say to me, "… what do you think?" What I discovered, over the course of many years, is that, more often than not, my head coach, as well as my assistant coaches, offered some very insightful comments that were extremely relevant concerning our own strengths and weaknesses, with regard to our efforts to win an upcoming game. This feedback occurred whether the coaches were young or old, veteran or rookie. One key belief that I have personally adhered to many, many times, over the years, is that there is never a "… dumb idea." In reality, turning an idea or a situation around 180 degrees might just be what the offense, defense, and special teams needed.

Watch the End Zone Close Copy of the Opponent's Defensive Line

After the exercise of watching the first half of a full game copy of our upcoming opponent with the entire staff, I, personally, as the offensive coordinator, would then study the end-zone-close copy of the upcoming team's defensive line with our offensive line coach. What I wanted to see was how formidable our upcoming opponent's defensive line was. It is my belief that quality defenses have quality defensive fronts. In turn, quality defensive fronts entail quality defensive linemen. Don't get me wrong. I believe that linebacker and secondary play are just as important as defensive line play. I still firmly believe, however, that winning football games all starts out in the trenches.

I always felt our offensive line could well handle a defensive line that had only one dominant defensive lineman. If our opponent had two quality defensive linemen, then we were facing a heavy chore. Three of four quality defensive linemen usually meant we were in for a heck of a fight. A basic part of our total offensive attack plan would then focus on negating the effectiveness of the outstanding defensive line first and foremost.

How do you attack defenses that have dominant defensive line personnel? First of all, you should utilize fast, quick-hitting run plays in which the offensive line wouldn't have to hold their blocks for an extended period of time. You should also focus on angle blocking, in which the dominant defensive linemen would be down- or out-blocked, rather than attempting to take them head on. In that regard, trap blocking can be extremely effective working with such down- or out-blocking action.

Double-team blocking is another way to negate quality defensive line play. As such, power run plays are an excellent means of utilizing double-teams and down- and out-blocking, along with linemen who pull and work up to the second level to block linebackers. Draws can also be very effective, as an offensive lineman delivers a hard, stunning-type block and then runs the defensive linemen up field to the side of the defender's rush effort.

Double- and triple-option action can be very effective versus quality defensive linemen. Option action forces defenses to be assignment-oriented. As a result, a defensive lineman can be slowed down in the execution of his assignments, which can take away some of his speed and aggressiveness.

The pass game must be thrown quickly. In other words, to have a realistic chance for a quarterback to complete passes consistently against quality defensive line pass rushers, the football must speedily come out of the quarterback's hand. Not only do passes thrown promptly help get the football out of the quarterback's hand quickly, they also help to tire defensive linemen. In that regard, draws, screens, quick passes, and quick screens, as well as actions that move the quarterback to allow him to throw on the run (sprint-out and move-out, nakeds, bootlegs and waggles) can all be helpful in tiring a defensive lineman, in a concerted effort to help make him less effective.

Tiring out big, quality defensive linemen is definitely a major key when facing such overbearing player threats. No-huddle offenses are also a great way to wear out quality defensive line play in an effort to negate the quality of play of the defensive linemen. Not surprisingly, throwing passes quickly makes it very difficult for defensive linemen to get to the quarterback, either to hinder his passing motion or register a sack.

Do a Positive Play Analysis of the Upcoming Opponent

Another effective game week planning action point that can be very effective is to do a positive play analysis versus your upcoming weekly opponent. This undertaking is a game-planning project that I felt was extremely important, as the coordinator, to accomplish. Quite simply, the positive play analysis charted all of the successful (i.e., four positive yards for a run; five positive yards for a pass) offensive plays that were executed against this week's upcoming opponent's defense.

When conducting a positive play analysis, I would not account for short (one- to three-yard) gains that were in successful third- or fourth-and-short situations, even though those plays were effective in converting those critical short-yardage situations. I did this because I was more interested, at this point, in analyzing base par runs and passes. As such, I felt keeping successful, converted, short-yardage plays separate from the positive play analysis helped make the analysis more valid.

In reality, the type of positive, successful plays is actually what I would look for in the positive play analysis. In our offense, we might have a screen pass play or two or three.

Our screen passes, however, might be executed slightly different from the type of screen run by other teams addressed in the positive play analysis. The key, in this instance, is that screen plays, in general, hurt the upcoming opponent, slightly different or not.

What the offensive coordinator should be looking for is the number of such play-types that hurt the opponent—run or pass. He then looks at what plays are similar to plays in his run/pass arsenal and fit the ones he feels comfortable with in his game plan. All factors considered, such an analysis can have a positive impact on your role as an offensive play caller.

Help New/Younger Coaches, If Such Assistance Is Needed

As much as I enjoy the role of being an offensive coordinator, working side-by-side with hard-working assistant coaches, there definitely are situations that occur when I must take time to help a new/young assistant coach who has recently joined our staff. As a rule, a new coach is, usually, all-fired-up to jump into the fray and start coaching. On the other hand, no matter how knowledgeable and experienced a new coach on your staff might be, someone (typically, the offensive coordinator) must lend a hand to help him learn and understand your offense and the way you utilize and employ various elements to help make your offense go. From the design of the offense to the specific vocabulary of the offense to route depths to the way fundamentals are utilized in your offense, etc., etc., every coach recently joining your staff must learn your system as quickly and thoroughly as possible.

Who is going to help bring the new/young staff member sufficiently up-to-snuff to effectively help coach the position he is being assigned to coach? More often than not, the chances are that you, the coordinator—the boss of the offense—the leader of the offense, must take on the responsibility of getting your new assistant coach on track quickly and effectively. How are you going to find the time to take on such a role? In reality, there are only so many hours in a day. On the other hand, breaking in a new coach efficiently to handle the coaching of a specific offensive position must be done well and must be accomplished relatively quickly.

Fortunately, you have options with regard to freeing up time for yourself. For example, there is almost always someone on the offensive staff, often a veteran, well-experienced coach, who can step up and take on a greater, more inclusive, coaching role, with regard to preparing for an upcoming opponent. Giving that veteran coach an additional, important, game preparation task, so that you, as the offensive coordinator, are able to free up some important time to mentor, coach, and teach a new/young coach who has joined the staff can be a viable possibility. After all, who should better be able to help someone understand your team's offense, than you—the offensive coordinator?

CHAPTER 12
UTILIZING PERSONNEL AND FORMATION VARIATIONS

Utilizing personnel and formation variations has been an effective concept for many coaches throughout their coaching careers. Defenses don't want to have to worry about personnel variations and multiple formations, especially when multiple sets, shifts, and motions are involved. Defenders, especially linebackers, strong safety types, and even defensive linemen want to read and react in their efforts to get to the football fast and furiously. Using the same, few formations offensively with the same, consistent personnel plans is, often, what defenses hope to see.

A key line of thought, when using multiple personnel and formational set variations, is to have a relatively small run-game inventory and a tight, moderate amount for the overall pass-game action. Then, offensive coordinators can utilize the tight, easy-to-use formation, shift, and motion packages to enhance, or disguise, a condensed, but well-designed, run and pass game.

The end result is an offense that many defensive coaches believe is a very tough offense to defend, due to all of the multiplicity of personnel, formation, shift, motion, and set capabilities. As a consequence, the offense can run the same run or pass plays with different personnel plans, formations, shifts, and motions to disturb the reading and thinking of the defensive players. Much of the shifting and motioning is used to feign action away from the actual attack points of the run and pass plays of the offense. On other times, such personnel, formation, shift, and motion variations can be utilized to help enhance the effectiveness of the run or pass-attack action directly at the points of attack.

Of course, an offensive coordinator can, more simply, have his offense set up on the line of scrimmage with a limited number of basic, more traditional formations without personnel, shift, motion, and set variations and still be extremely successful. In reality, a number of offensive coordinators believe that being more basic and not using a multiplicity of personnel, formation, shifts, motion, and sets helps to produce a clearer picture of how the defense will line up and attempt to attack the offense in front of them. These offensive coordinators argue that less can mean more, with regard to having a more simple offense to execute. In addition, there can be a greater ability to use a quick snap count on such more static, basic formation thinking, which forces the defense to lock in to the reading of the offense immediately as it addresses the line of scrimmage.

Varied Personnel Usage

In fact, defenses do not want to see different personnel usage on every play or close to every play. They do not want to see two tight ends in 12 personnel, aligned in a wing set to the same side, and, suddenly, see a double-flip action to the opposite side of the formation and then have the wing-tight end motion back across the formation, after he has set himself for a full second. Diagram 12-1 illustrates such varied personnel usage, with combined shift and motion action.

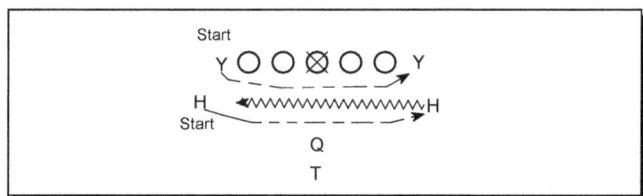

Diagram 12-1. (12 personnel) flipping two tight ends and then motioning the (H) wing tight end back across the formation

On the next play, the defense can see a 10 personnel, 2 x 2 formation, with the back shifting into a no-back formation, as shown in Diagram 12-2. Varying personnel usage, along with varied formations, motions, shifts, and sets, creates numerous possibilities for different and disguised offensive looks.

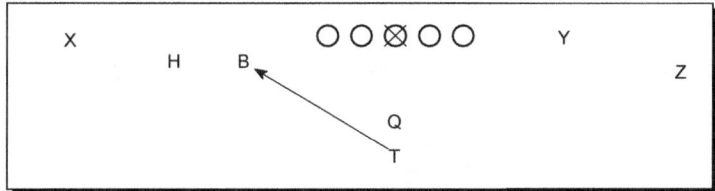

Diagram 12-2. (10 personnel) 2 x 2 formation, with the back shifting into a 3 x 2 no-back formation

Personnel Plan Numbering

A key to personnel plan usage is the simplicity of using meaningful personnel numbers. A basic, pro personnel plan is numbered "21"—two backs and one tight end. A "12" personnel numbering refers to one back and two tight ends. A "10" personnel numbering refers to one back and four wide receivers. Diagram 12-3 offers a personnel numbering chart to detail the fit of the numbers used in the personnel numbering system.

```
 0 personnel = 0 backs, 0 tight ends, 5 wide receivers
10 personnel = 1 back, 0 tight ends, 4 wide receivers
11 personnel = 1 back, 1 tight end, 3 wide receivers
12 personnel = 1 back, 2 tight ends, 2 wide receivers
13 personnel = 1 back, 3 tight ends, 1 wide receiver
14 personnel = 1 back, 4 tight ends, 0 wide receivers
20 personnel = 2 backs, 0 tight ends, 3 wide receivers
21 personnel = 2 backs, 1 tight end, 2 wide receivers
22 personnel = 2 backs, 2 tight ends, 1 wide receiver
```

Diagram 12-3. Personnel numbering chart

Why all this elaborate, varied personnel action? The reason is that the defense now has to realign properly versus such offensive personnel variation and change on a consistent basis. As a rule, this situation will often require new defensive communication right before the snap of the football. It also could entail the creation of a personnel mismatch of a specific offensive player aligned over a specific defender. Furthermore, it could mean a linebacker pointing out a shift or a motion to other defenders, rather than being settled in a gathered stance, ready to uncoil and strike. In fact, if the defense attempts to substitute with a substituted offender, who is running out on the field, defensive unsettledness and mistakes can easily occur.

Such personnel variation is neither difficult to understand or execute. Diagram 12-3 lists nine basic personnel plans. The key to personnel variation usage is focused practice. An offensive coordinator should not expect to smoothly execute personnel changes in a game, if he doesn't constantly practice such substitution action on a consistent basis.

Anytime an offense engages in a full team drill is an excellent opportunity to practice personnel variation calls and changes. In reality, the popularly used 7-on-7 pass drill is also an excellent way to practice such personnel substitution. The only problem with such full team or 7-on-7 personnel substitution practice action (and varying formations, shifts, motions, and sets) is that the coaches who signal in the formations and play calls in games must also do so from the sideline in practice.

Varied Formational Usage

The next premise to be examined is the possibility of varying your formational usage. Presenting a defense with a different type of formation from the play you just previously used can do a lot to disturb a defense, with regard to its recognition abilities and/or with the task of proper alignment. A simple, easy-to-use system of executing such a variety of formations (along with the possibility of using personnel variations at the same time) can work to substantially disturb a defense. For example, an offensive coordinator could use three different formations in a row when play calling, while utilizing one personnel plan for all three. On the other hand, the offensive coordinator could utilize three different personnel plans for each of those three separate run or pass plays. The main point, in this instance, is that the offensive coordinator could make a variety of run or pass play calls from a variety of personnel plans and formations.

Varied Sets, Shifts, and Motions

To this point, this chapter has addressed the use of a variety of runs and passes from a variety of personnel plans and formations. The next step is to add the usage of sets, shifts, and motions to help create an even greater multiple offensive attack.

Sets are, simply, the alignment positions that an offensive back (including the quarterback), wide receivers, and tight ends can take prior to the snap of the football. Such sets either can be in fixed positions prior to the snap of the football or can be dummy positions, awaiting for a shift call or signal to get moved to the desired formational alignment prior to the snap of the football. A set is a common, abbreviated call for a positional alignment. Diagram 12-4 details examples a variety of sets for the ("B") running backs, ("Y") tight ends, and the ("W") wide receivers.

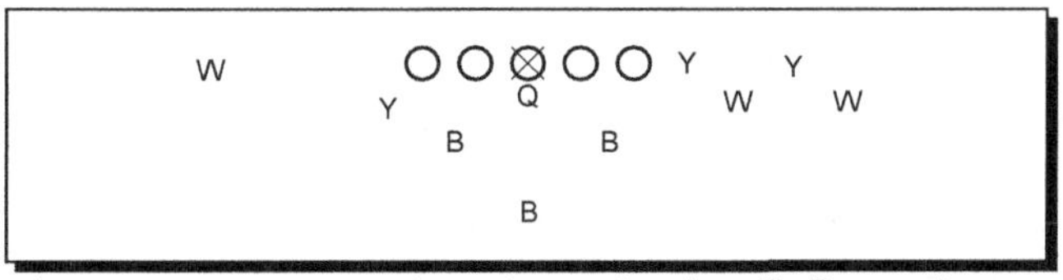

Diagram 12-4. Examples of sets for the ("B") running backs, the ("Y") tight ends, and the ("W") wide receivers

Shifts are nothing more than the movement of a ("B") running back, a ("Y") tight end, or a ("W") wide receiver from one, set, positional alignment to another set. This movement is undertaken in an effort to get some form of alignment advantage or to feign a dummy, false-action that gets defenders' eyes and focus away from the actual offensive point of attack.

Most defenses don't fear simple backfield sets until such sets shift from one side of a formation to the other, changing the player strength of the formation. On the other hand, offensive backs, shifting from one side of a formation to the other, is commonly carried out to attain a more desired, or disguised, run threat set or a more favorable side from which to block, be it a run or pass play.

All-in-all, defenses seem more concerned with tight end and wide receiver shifts undertaken in an effort to outflank frontal defenders, as well as the changing of strengths of the formation from one side of the formation to the other, than they are offensive backs. Such tight end shift actions are also utilized by wide receivers. As a rule, however, offensive coordinators seem to employ motion actions to a greater degree by wide receivers rather than shifts. Diagram 12-5 shows examples of offensive back, tight end, and wide receiver shift actions.

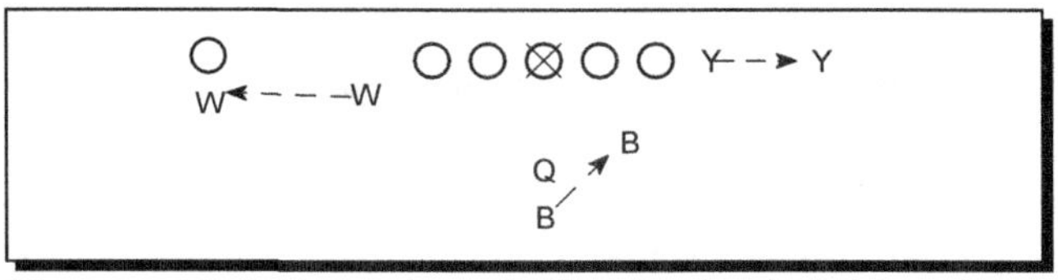

Diagram 12-5. Examples of offensive back, tight end, and wide receiver shift actions

As has already been stated, offensive multiplicity can be an extremely effective way to produce dynamic, high-scoring, offensive production. A major key to being effective with a multiple personnel, formation, shift, motion, and set, however, is to be sure to have a tightly designed, easy-to-use, multiple offense, with a limited amount of integral, multiple offense parts.

Wide receiver motion is, for the most part, the most commonly employed and most commonly noticed motion action. Wide receiver motions are able to distort both the zone and man pass coverages of the defensive secondary and quickly change the strength of a formation. As such, they help to produce effective zone passing angles and windows, as well as man-to-man pass-game match-ups. Wide receiver run motion also helps to make it difficult for a pass defender to jam a wide receiver and/or disrupt the wide receiver's pass release and route.

Wide receiver motion actions can greatly help a coordinator and the wide receivers to determine whether the pass coverage being utilized is a man-to-man or a zone coverage, while on the run. With rare exceptions, if a secondary pass defender runs across the formation to cover a cross-the-formation, motioning wide receiver, the pass coverage is a man-to-man coverage. Diagram 12-6 illustrates cross-the-formation wide receiver motion action versus man-to-man coverage.

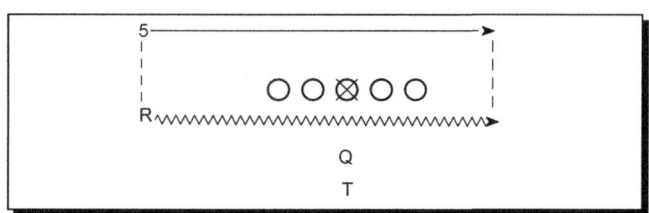

Diagram 12-6. Cross-the-formation wide receiver
motion versus man-to-man coverage

If the secondary follows and covers the cross-the-formation wide receiver with a bumping-across action of the second-level defenders, the pass coverage is, most likely, a zone coverage. Diagram 12-7 shows a zone bumping coverage action versus a crossing wide receiver.

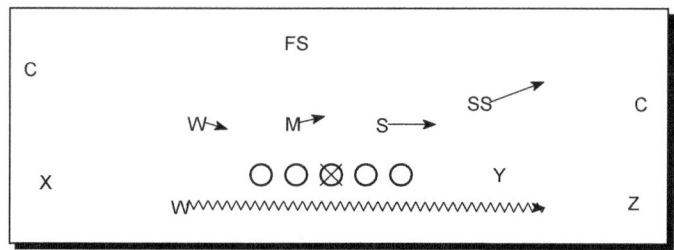

Diagram 12-7. Cross-the-formation wide receiver motion
versus zone coverage

Tight end motions are extremely effective in their ability to quickly change the strength of a formation by motioning from one side of a formation to the other. Tight end return motion, in which a tight end motions past the center and turns 180 degrees to work back to his original side, helps to create distortion and uncertainty for the defense. Along with short motion, all three variations of tight end motion can help to put the tight ends in excellent alignment positions to be effective blockers or pass receivers. Tight end motions can be helped on their pass releases by motion action. The reason for this factor is that a defender must deal with and negotiate a moving target on the tight end's release efforts.

Running back motions have become increasingly utilized in offenses in recent years. This factor has been especially true with the increase of empty/no-back personnel plans and formations. Ten-personnel four wide receivers and 11-personnel three wide receivers, one tight end formations can quickly become empty/no-back formations with running back lateral motions toward the sidelines. Diagram 12-8 shows the use of running back motion to help create an empty/no-back formation.

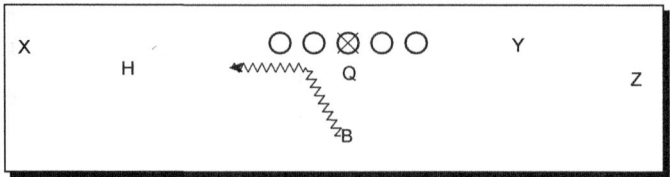

Diagram 12-8. Running back lateral motion to create an empty/no-back formation

CHAPTER 13
PLANNING THE PAR (BASE) OFFENSE

It's Monday of a Friday night game week. As a result, Monday and Tuesday practices are, usually, the heavy, fully geared, practice days. Mondays and Tuesdays are when the majority of the game plan is introduced to the players and practiced. I have always felt that the planning and focus of Monday practices should be on par (base) down offense and third-down offense. (Third-down offense planning will be discussed in Chapter 14.)

Another term commonly used for par down offense is base offense, the "basic" runs and passes that make up the core of your offense—the portion of your offense that the remainder of your offensive play needs to build around. Much of the remainder of your offense's run and pass inventory should, then, become run and pass plays that you feel are additionally necessary for game-specific situations, such as third-down, red zone, and goal line offense. As such, as a rule, par, or base, down offense should normally act as the starting point, or the fundamental source, of a team's total offensive attack plan.

Par (Base) Down Game Planning

Par (base) run and pass offense should be the hub of the offense … the foundation … the center … the heart. When someone asks an offensive coordinator what type of offense he runs, the answer lies in the word, or words, that describe the base offense being utilized by his team. The base, or par, offense includes the key running game plays, whether they are hand-off runs or run/keep/option-type plays. As far as the pass game, the key pass plays can be anything from quick, three-step dropback passes to five- and, possibly, seven-step dropback passes. On the other hand, the key base passes can also be any kind of move or sprint-out passes, play-action passes, or misdirection-type passes such as nakeds, bootlegs, or waggles.

Most par (base) down situations are normally considered first down, second-and-medium, and second-and-short. Second-and-long situations, for the most part, entail a slightly different thought process, attempting to gain at least three to five yards to put the offense in a workable third-and-short or third-and-medium situation.

The offensive coordinator should treat par (base) down offense as he does any other key, game-specific situation. Who should do the scouting analysis of the opponent's defensive game video? Who should put together the proposal of the runs and passes to be used in par (base) down situations? In that regard, deciding how to address these questions is the responsibility of the offensive coordinator.

In reality, there may be a veteran coach on the offensive staff with whom the coordinator feels comfortable, with regard to handling both the par (base) down run and pass games. In turn, the coordinator might decide to have the offensive line coach and the quarterback coach work together, with the line coach working on the par (base) run game and the quarterback coach working on the par (base) pass game. On the other hand, the offensive coordinator might assign this portion of the game plan to himself, given that par (base) down offense is so important to the overall effectiveness of the offense.

The assigned par (base) down "specialist" is responsible for a listing of the specific par (base) down run and pass plays, with the accompanied, desired personnel plan, formations, and possible, sets, shifts, and motions. The par (base) down specialist must be sure to list the formations and plays properly on the play call chart in relation to hash mark and midfield positional considerations.

How many times should the assigned par (base) down specialist list a particular run or pass play? The answer depends on the number of possible effective run and pass plays the specialist feels he has in his arsenal. Is there a run that is the offense's signature run, perhaps an inside zone run play? He should, probably, list such a play two, or three, times from varied personnel, formational, shifts, and motions to make it difficult for a defense to lock in to specific personnel and formational looks that might tip off such a play.

Should a coordinator repeat a particular run, or pass, play that was just successful? The answer is probably not. A play that was just successful is what will most be on a defender's mind as he aligns for the next play. A different play call should be made with the thought of coming back to that particular successful play, after the next preceding, varied play. What if that particular offensive play is overpowering, and the defense just doesn't seem to be able to handle the play's effectiveness? Then, run it again—and again—and again!

Diagram 13-1 illustrates a sample par (base) down play call chart. Run plays are listed first, with pass plays listed underneath the run plays.

❏ Runs:

(11) Pistol Deuce Lt 40
(11) Pistol Deuce Lt Z Fly Sweep RT
(12) Wing Lt Twins 20 Read Option
(12) Doubles Lt Zone Check
(11) Zoom Trips Lt 20 RPO
(12) Wing Rt Whip 8 Stretch
(12) Wing Lt Twins Zip-Zap 2 Lead
 (0) Nobs Lt QB Draw
(11) Doubles Rt S Fly 20 Trap
(11) Zoom Trips Lt 6 Counter

(11) Pistol Deuce Rt 41
(11) Pistol Deuce Rt Fly Sweep Lt
(12) Wing Rt Twins 21 Read Option
(12) Doubles Rt Zone Check
(11) Zoom Trips Rt 21 RPO
(12) Wing Lt Whip 9 Stretch
(12) Wing Rt Twins Zip-Zap 3 Lead
 (0) Nobs Rt QB Draw
 (0) Doubles Lt S Fly 21 Trap
(11) Zoom Trips Rt 7 Counter

❏ Passes:

(11) Zap Wing Lt Deuce 33 Y-Out
(11) Trey Rt 24 Naked Lt
(21) Weak Pro Rt 71 F Angle
(11) Weak Trips Lt Sprint Rt Flood
(10) Pistol Trey Rt 260 Verts
(10) Pistol Doubles Lt 250 X-Ray

(11) Zap Wing Rt Deuce 32 Y-Out
(11) Trey Lt 25 Naked Rt
(11) Weak Pro Lt 70 F Angle
(11) Weak Trips Rt Sprint Lt Flood
(10) Pistol Trey Lt 160 Verts
(10) Pistol Doubles Rt 150 X-Ray

Diagram 13-1. Sample par (base) down play call chart

It is important to make sure that whatever the run and pass plays are on the par (base) down play call chart that there is a balance of attack. In your first three weeks of the season, your counter run or pass actions may not have been very successful. If such plays are truly a basic part of your run or pass play offensive design, you should make sure that such key, basic plays are still on the par (base) play call chart and have been practiced to the point that they are game ready. Why? Because if the defense is successfully overloading to your normally effective inside and outside zone run plays, you may suddenly find that those counter runs or counter naked/bootleg pass plays may suddenly become extremely effective.

Many coaches will state that their par (base) down offense game plan is already set from week to week in the form of their pre-established base offensive package that should have been carefully developed in the off-season. After all, base offense is the central, core part of a team's offense. There are a number of ways that a particular par (base) down play, however, such as an off-tackle power play, can be run versus a specific defense as a result of personnel and formation usage. The key is for the offensive coordinator or offensive specialist to determine which way they will run such a power play with all of these personnel and formational variations to augment such a base run play.

Some coaches state that their par (base) down offensive game plan is easy to establish from week-to-week, "… just utilize your already established base offensive package and use that each week versus all opponents." In my opinion, these coaches need to "… be careful." Some of the plays on their pre-established par (base) down offense just might not work well against a specific opponent.

For example, post-corner smash pass patterns will probably have little success action versus a three-deep, cover 3 opponent. Yes, they might get a lot of short throws underneath to the short, hitch-type under route of the smash pattern concept. On the other hand, they could simply throw to hitch/under routes quickly for the same successful, short gain versus such a three-deep coverage using quick, three-step timed quick throws, without the much more delayed, five-step to seven-step deep smash pass pattern concept and its slower developing action. Diagram 13-2 details how to smartly throw to a hitch route off of quick, three-step timing, rather than to a slow, high/low smash read versus a three-deep, cover 3 coverage.

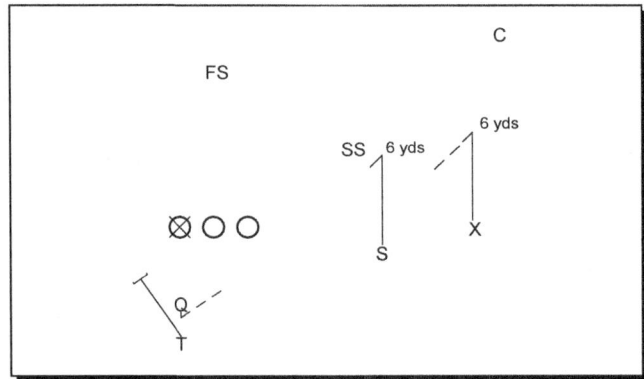

Diagram 13-2. Throwing a quick, three-step timed hitch route, instead of an under/hitch portion of a five- to seven-step smash route pattern versus cover 3

Yes, the bulk of your par (base) down plays should come from your base down offense that you established in the off-season. On the other hand, it must be your best par (base) down plays, utilizing your best runs and passes from your best personnel and formational actions. Such a plan gives you the opportunity to use your best run and pass plays to attack a defense's weaknesses and/or use your par (base) down personnel and formation actions to create such defensive weaknesses.

Addressing Second-and-Long Situations

Most par (base) down situations are normally considered first-down, second-and-medium, and second-and-short situations. Second-and-long situations (i.e., eight or more yards) entail a different thought process than other second-down situations. Many offensive coordinators, feeling a bit stuck with second-and-long situations, attempt to gain at least four to five yards to put the offense in a workable third-and-short or third-and-medium situation in the offense's effort to gain a new first down. In such action, gaining four or five yards on second-and-long puts an offense into a more workable position for third-down yardage needs.

The word "manageable" is a key consideration for second-and-long situations. In these circumstances, the most pressing issue for the offense is that defenses can command a greater deal of defensive play-calling variations (e.g., nickel-and-dime coverages and blitz-action), compared to more normal par (base) down situations. Accordingly, second-and-long offenses might be wise to run the football utilizing their best, most efficient, run plays.

When facing a second-and-long situation, a reasonable second-and-long run play of four to five yards can greatly help to set up manageable third-down yardage situations. Quick dives, draws, and trap-type plays can help a back pop through the defense to help set up sizable, manageable third-down gains or even achieve all of the second-and-long yardage needs. Another alternative you have is to, simply, run the best, or one of the best, run plays from your par (base) down arsenal to gain the desired yardage to, again, put your offense in a manageable, third-and-short yardage situation. Furthermore, you should also be aware that certain run-option plays can create offensive overloads with which the outside perimeter defenders must contend.

The defensive focus of second-and-long situations can be pointed toward defensive fronts and coverages that are designed to stop the pass game, especially the short pass game. Blitzes, stunts, nickel, and dime coverages are but a few of the measures a defense might utilize to prevent a second-and-long offense from being successful in gaining a first down or putting the offense into a manageable third-down situation.

As such, the offense can utilize short, quick, three-step timed passes to help gain needed medium-short yardage to put the offense in the more manageable third-down situation scenario. The other positive for using the short, quick pass game is that it is an excellent blitz-beater weapon, helping the offense to negate successful blitz-action by the defense. Quick play-action passes and naked/bootleg-type passes are also excellent types of pass plays that can help the offense to gain the necessary short yardage needed to set up a manageable, needed third-down yardage situation. The same factor can be said for quick-developing screen plays. Diagram 13-3 provides a sample second-and-long play call chart.

❒ Runs:	
(12) Strong Lt Twins 35 Power	(12) Strong Rt Twins 36 Power
(12) Unbalanced Rt Speed Option Lt	(12) Unbalanced Lt Speed Option Rt
(10) Pistol Deuce Lt 41 Trap	(10) Pistol Deuce Rt 40 Trap
(11) Pistol Trey Rt Sprint Draw Lt	(11) Pistol Trey Lt Sprint Draw Rt
❒ Passes:	
(12) Wing Twins Lt Bend/Slants	(12) Wing Twins Rt Bend/Slants
(11) Trey Rt 20 Speed-Out RPO	(12) Trey Lt 21 Speed-Out RPO

Diagram 13-3. Sample second-and-long play call chart

Scouting the Opponent's Defense Analytically

How does the par (base) down situation specialist decide which plays (with personnel and formational considerations) to use in this portion of his, hopefully, successful total, attacking game plan? That decision comes from the careful analysis given to him by his computer and the analytical, scouting breakdown report program he is using.

Such computer usage enables the offensive coordinator to see how a defense is going to try to stop his style of offense attack. It will also provide breakdowns of the type of fronts he needs to block, including the type of stunts and blitzes he will see come game time. Furthermore, it will help him decide what type of passing will best attack the opponent's par (base) down defense. All-in-all, play-action passing, especially nakeds and bootlegs, are excellent in this situation. The same factor also holds true for quick, three-step passing.

Balance is an important part of par (base) down offense. As a result, dropback and move/sprint-out-type passing should also be included to round out an offense's total balance needs. In addition, the offensive coordinator should never dismiss the possibility of pounding the football with his best run-game plays.

In reality, the aforementioned may sound like a lot of offense for such a game-specific situation, such as second-and-long. On the other hand, that's why a team's par (base) down offensive play ready list should be tight and condensed.

Create a Tight, Uncluttered Par (Base) Down Situational Plan

Once again, you should have a tightly condensed, relatively small, par (base) down situational plan. In reality, you should, probably, not have every par (base) down run or pass play in your total arsenal on a game day, par (base) down play call list. Your play call list should have your best runs and passes on it. You should use the plays that jump out at you when you cull the total list of par (base) down runs and plays. If you have to ask yourself "… should I? … or … shouldn't I? … put such a play on my par (base) down play call list," you should eliminate that play. By using this line of questioning, when deciding what to have on your par (base) down offense game plan list, you'll more than likely find out that you will have your bread-and-butter par (base) down plays, as well as a few, important, key supportive plays.

A condensed list also allows for a greater amount of practice time per play. As such, the following previously mentioned concept should be kept in mind, "what you do is important, however, how you do what you do is far more important!" As such, you should make sure that your par (base) down plan is manageable … that you have time to get your par (base) down plan well-practiced, rather than have a diluted, overburdened plan. As a rule, you should be wary of installing new plays. New plays typically mean they've had three to four days of practice to become game-ready. That scenario can be quite scary, especially early in the season, since the rest of your total offense still has so much teaching, coaching, and practice to do.

CHAPTER 14
PLANNING THE THIRD-DOWN OFFENSE

Although this factor could be definitely well-debated, the most important portion of game planning and its resultant game-plan practice work is third-down offense. Why is third-down offense so important to start its planning and practice on a Monday alongside par, base down offense? Arguably, because third-down offense is extremely critical to an offense's efforts to consistently move the football down the field and score points.

Failure to convert on third down will, normally, force an offense to give up possession of the football, rather than successfully continuing to move it down the field in an effort to score a touchdown or, at a minimum, kick a field goal. In reality, successfully, or unsuccessfully, succeeding in the critical situations of the red zone, on the goal line, on two-minute offense drives, on four-minute slowdown drives, and in coming-out situations is often dependent on how well an offense is at converting on third down for it to be successful.

Furthermore, by focusing in on third-down offense on the earliest, heavily padded practice day of the week, an extra day of third-down offense and, as a result, possible blitz pick-up practice needs, enables a team to give much needed attention to protecting the quarterback in passing situations. To stop or, at least, control a defense's blitz pressure efforts takes a tremendous amount of game practice, game performance focus, and concerted game planning. To be successful in converting key third-down situations, an offense must be able to pick up the blitz and all other forms of pass-game pressure in the defense's efforts to sack or otherwise disturb a quarterback's passing attempts. In addition, having a sound blitz pick-up package can often result in big plays for the offense, if the offense can exploit weaknesses in a defense's blitz and blitz-coverage efforts.

Successfully converting key third-down situations innately produces a positive, uplifting feeling of achievement, as the offense sees the down-and-distance, yard-marker chains effectively moving forward toward the goal line in their ongoing quest to score points. In turn, unsuccessfully converting key third-down situations produces negative, failure-induced feelings of disappointment and, possibly, despair, as the offense trudges off the field, hearing the boisterous, excited howls of the opposing defense as it forces a change in ball possession. In this instance, the offense loses momentum, as the defense gains it.

More often than not, all of these factors are a defining reason for why a team may win, or lose, a game. If an offensive coordinator checks his previous season's third-down success percentages for each game, he will often find a direct correlation between his third-down convergence success percentage and his team's actual game win/loss record.

Make Third-Down Yardage Routes Work

In reality, third-down game situations almost have a world of their own, with regard to play-call selections. The factor that makes third-down offense so special is, of course, that every third-down situation has its own yardage parameter that the offense must reach to successfully convert the third-down situation at hand. As a result, completing a six-yard hitch route to a wide receiver could, very likely, mean failure on a third-and-eight down-and-distance situation, if a cornerback is able to immediately make a tackle on the hitch-catching wide receiver for only a six-yard gain.

What should have happened in the aforementioned situation would have been for the offensive coordinator to have the quarterback throw a short, 12-back-to-10-yard acute route (a short comeback route). An acute route reception of the short comeback route would, in itself, most likely enable the acute route receiver to catch the football and gain at least 9 to 10 yards. Such an acute route catch would, most likely, be successful, even if the receiver was tackled immediately, or if he ran out of bounds.

The rationale to this example is that the offensive coordinator should not call for specific pass routes that, in themselves, will have a tough time gaining the necessary third-down yardage needs. Rather, he should call routes that have a strong possibility of converting the third-down situation upon the completion of the pass. Diagram 14-1 shows the comparison of a hitch route and an acute route completion in relation to the line-to-gain marker.

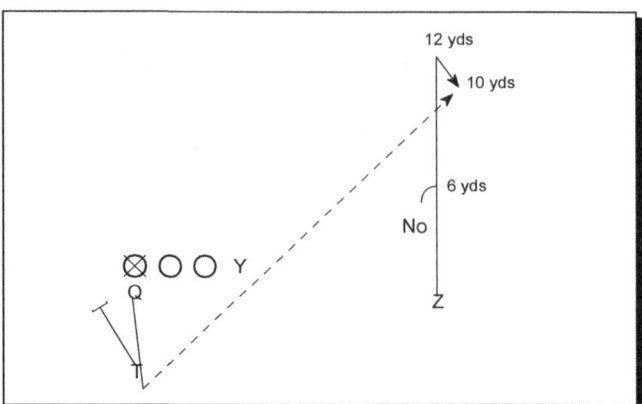

Diagram 14-1. Using a 12-to-10 acute route to gain
third and eight yards, rather than a six-yard hitch route

The aforementioned example does not hold true for all pass routes. The slant route is an example of how a quick, pass game, three-step timed quarterback pass can turn into successful longer yardage play, due to its design of catching the football on the run and quickly working up the field vertically. Diagram 14-2 illustrates how a quick, three-step timed pass-drop throw can turn a short, slant route into a substantial amount of upfield, vertical run distance.

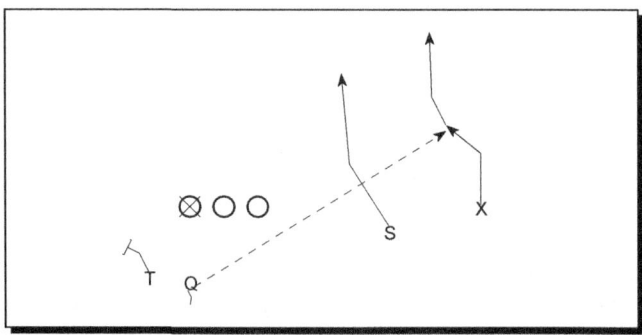

Diagram 14-2. Example of a quick slant route turning
into a longer yardage play

Analyzing the Opponent's Third-Down Defensive Tendencies

In the previous section of this chapter, it was noted what type of plays, run or pass, would give an offense the chance to get the yardage needed to convert a specific third-down situation. At this point, it is time to analyze the actual defensive fronts, coverages, stunts, and blitzes that the opposing defenses will utilize in their efforts to prevent the offense from converting new first-and-10 situations.

In reality, such opponent third-down analyses are, quite frankly, a 180-degree flip of the efforts of the offense in the offense's efforts to keep themselves on the field with fresh, new sets of downs. The defenses will plot game plans against any of the tendencies shown by the offense as seen on scouting video. For example, if the offense has run the football on third-and-short (one to two yards) 16 of 17 times, the chances are that the defense will counter the offense's efforts by beefing up their defensive front to stop the run. This factor should suggest to the offensive coordinator to consider calling some form of quick developing, play-action pass to the outside in an effort to out-flank a beefed-up defensive front.

In a similar vein, if, on third and seven to nine yards, the offense is 10 for 11 throwing the football, the offensive coordinator should expect to see the nickel and dime type coverages and/or blitz and line game pressures to negate the extensive use of the pass game in this critical third-down game situation. Does the opponent play man-to-man coverage, zone coverage, or a mixture of both? Video breakdown analysis can be utilized to find the tendencies (which there almost always are) of the opposing defense in those third-down situations. Furthermore, the offensive coordinator should think about breaking the offense's 10-for-11 pass tendency with a draw, a quick-hitting trap play, a sweep, or a run-option play. If all of the passes have been dropback passes, the offense could use move-out, roll-out, or sprint-out passes to break the tendency of having the quarterback drop straight back on all 11 passes. As a rule, such a change of the quarterback's pass launch point can greatly disrupt the defense's pass rush and pressure attempts.

A big key to successful third-down offense is to find ways to vary the offense's third-down situation game plans. As such, the offense should not be predictable. It should make sure it still uses some varied personnel plans, formations, sets, shifts, and motions to help keep the third-down defensive efforts in abeyance. On the other hand, don't be afraid. For example, if a defense can't stop the offense's read-option play or an outside zone run play on third-and-medium (three to six yards), the offense should run it, again and again and again!

Third-and-Short (One to Two Yards) Game Plan

As a result of yardage needs to convert third-down yardage situations, there needs to be established yardage delineations. Such third-down delineations can vary from one offensive coordinator to another. Most coaches will start out with a third-and-short delineation meaning third and one to two yards.

Obviously, running the ball is a major consideration on third-and-short (one to two yards). The offensive coordinator should, initially, cull his running game list from his par (base) down offensive planning. For example, are there runs in the par (base) down offensive list that would make for good power running versus an, often, beefed-up, short-yardage defense? Or, are there any explosive goal line run plays that could fit the offensive coordinator's third-and-short offensive attack needs?

Option runs can be also extremely effective from heavy personnel formations, as well as from par (base) down offense. The same factor can be true for sweep runs. In fact, a number of coaches feel that spread option offense action is an excellent means of attacking third-and-short defenses. Of course, double and triple option offensive attacks, such as the wishbone or an offense from an I formation, are excellent alternatives for gaining necessary short-yardage needs.

Many coaches feel that running the football is the way to go on short yardage (one to two yards) situations. Such a belief is particularly viable, if a team has a strong offensive line, or if the team it is facing does not have a stout defensive front. Finding, and exploiting, third-and-short defensive front weaknesses is another reason for trying to develop a complete understanding of how to best utilize the run game. Furthermore, run/pass options (RPOs) can definitely tie together a team's par (base) down runs with its quick pass game.

In addition to RPOs, the offensive coordinator should also not forget the pass game on third-and-short situations. A quick, three-step drop completion to a wide receiver or a tight end will almost always produce the needed short yardage. Moreover, the quickness of the delivery of a three-step timed hitch or quick-out makes it extremely tough for the defense to get to the quarterback in time to sack him, or put duress on him.

Move passes, such as sprint-out, roll-out, bootleg, naked bootleg, and waggle-type passing, are also an excellent means of successfully gaining needed short yardage. Such pass-actions should be designed to give the quarterback a quick, open throw to receivers who are stretching the defensive coverage out toward the flat.

As in all throwing actions to receivers, whether versus man-to-man or zone coverages, the offensive coordinator needs to game plan third-and-short passes that best attack the defensive coverages used by the opponent in such situations. Accordingly, if the third-and-short defenses employ a mixture of man-to-man and zone pass coverages, the coordinator must be sure to call for pass patterns that can readily attack both pass coverage concepts. In addition, all factors considered, if the pass-action used is a quick, sprint-out pass, the quarterback has an excellent chance to gain the needed third-and-short yardage by running the football for a first down.

"Balance ..." should definitely be a key factor when considering whether to make a third-and-short run or pass play call. As such, an offensive coordinator should call the play, or plays, that he feels will be successful, whether those plays are runs or passes. On the other hand, an appropriate balance of both runs and passes for third-and-short situations is also an important factor.

A third-and-short offense should be sure to utilize a blend of both runs and passes, so that the third-and-short defenses have to be concerned about both facets of the game. Furthermore, if the safeties are brought down in their alignment to almost act as extra linebackers, the offensive coordinator should not be stubborn and still try to pound the football, when other less stringent play-call options are available. Gaining needed third-and-short yardage is the goal whether via the air or on the ground. Diagram 14-3 provides an example of a third-and-short (one to two yards) play-call chart.

<table>
<tr><td colspan="2">❏   Runs:</td></tr>
<tr><td>(12) Double Wing Lt QB Sneak</td><td>(12) Double Wing Rt QB Sneak</td></tr>
<tr><td>(13) Gun Strong Wing Rt Tight 38 QB</td><td>(13) Gun Strong Wing Lt Tight 39 QB</td></tr>
<tr><td>(12) Zoom I Lt Twins 37 Power</td><td>(12) Zoom I Rt Twins 36 Power</td></tr>
<tr><td colspan="2"> </td></tr>
<tr><td colspan="2">❏   Passes:</td></tr>
<tr><td>(12) Yac I Deuce Lt 92 Chop</td><td>(12) Yac I Deuce Rt 93 Chop</td></tr>
<tr><td>(10) Strong Rt Trey Sprint Rt Flood</td><td>(10) Strong Lt Trey Sprint Lt Flood</td></tr>
<tr><td>(10) Yac Doubles Rt 90 Hitch</td><td>(10) Yac Doubles Lt 90 Hitch</td></tr>
</table>

Diagram 14-3. An example of a third-and-short play-call chart

Third-and-Medium (Three to Six Yards) Game Plan

Third-and-medium (three to six yards) is often called the "… manageable …" third-down situation. In reality, third-and-short (one to two yards) situational offense, for the most part, is not usually considered a manageable third down by many coaches. The reason for this attitude is because of the considerable personnel and formational investments made by both the offense and the defense, in the offense's efforts to gain enough vital yards to convert the third-and-short situation and in the defense's efforts to prevent it from occurring. As a result, "heavy" personnel and overloaded run game efforts can create a separate, or special category of its own—the already discussed third down-and-short yardage situation.

Third-and-medium (three to six yards) is considered a manageable third-down situation, because the dual threat possibility of both an offense's run and pass games. As such, the offensive coordinator should feel that he's totally in control to use his best run and pass plays to gain needed third-and-medium yardage. An offense's run game can gain needed first-down yardage on the ground for three or four yards and, even, five or six, in a given scenario in which an offense's par (base) down offense can be readily utilized. Furthermore, when putting the football in the air, there is an excellent opportunity to use most anything a coordinator might want to call from his pass game arsenal, just as long as he feels that the quarterback can be properly protected to get the pass thrown effectively.

Quick-hitting, straight-ahead run plays can be very effective on third-and-medium situations. With the possibility of defensive penetration of the line of scrimmage efforts, quick traps can be especially effective, as can quick-hitting draw plays. Down block, kick-out run plays and power run plays can also help control penetrating defensive fronts. In addition, counter and reverse-type plays can be extremely effective, as long as the offensive line can prevent defensive, line-of-scrimmage penetration. Since counters and reverses are usually complementary run plays, great faking of prime run-game plays can help to make the counters and reverses all the more effective, given that third-and-medium defenders are, usually, focusing on such initial, prime run-play action.

Furthermore, sweeps and run-option plays, whether they are double or triple options, can be extremely effective on third-and-medium offensive situations. In addition, the currently widely utilized spread, run-option plays are hard to defend on third-and-medium situations. In that regard, sweeps can be excellent third down-and-medium play calls for a coordinator, if the sweep plays can fully account for all perimeter and end-of-line defenders. Just as in third-and-short situations, RPOs (run/pass options) can also be extremely effective on third-and-medium play-call situations.

Pass-game usage possibilities in third-and-medium situations are excellent. The key words with regard to the pass game on third-and-medium situations should be "get completions." In reality, however, if on a three-tiered flood route pattern, the quarterback sees that the outside streak route is wide open, he should go-for-broke. On the other hand, if the down-the-field route reads are not wide open, he should just get completions. For example, the quarterback should throw the football to the flat route, stretching to the sideline.

As a rule, completions have a great tendency of gaining third-and-medium yardage needs, and often, more. As such, the quarterback must not takes chances on throwing for a few extra yards, if he has a wide open, short-route completion possibility that, in itself, will produce the needed third-and-medium yardage. Again, his underlying, overriding mentality should be to get completions. Diagram 14-4 illustrates how a quick throw to the flat route can get the needed, third down-and-medium yardage, as well as a new set of downs, employing a flood pattern principle.

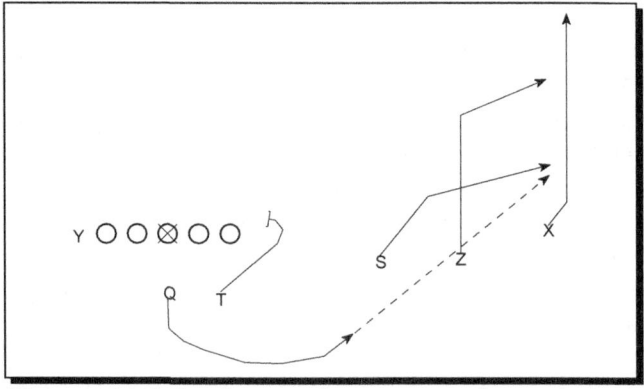

Diagram 14-4. Passing to a flat route to gain needed first-down yardage

Quick, three-step timed quarterback pass-actions also have an excellent chance of gaining needed first-down yardage on a third-and-medium down-and-distance situation. As such, hitches, quick-outs, and slants are excellent play calls for an offensive coordinator. If the offensive coordinator adds some quick, play-action passes in his arsenal in these situations to help influence the linebacker/strong safety defenders, he will often be able to find big holes in the defense's pass coverage attempts to cover such quickly timed pass routes.

Sprint-out actions are another viable choice for a coordinator to call on third-and-medium situations. The main reason for this factor is the quarterback's ability to run for needed first-down yardage, if the pass routes of the pass pattern that were called seem to be well-covered. As such, the defense is put into a dilemma. Do pass coverage defenders leave the receivers they are covering on a sprint-out type pass action in an attempt to tackle the quarterback, leaving the vacated receiver open to receive a first-down yardage pass?

Bootleg, naked bootleg, and waggle-type play-action passes are also very good third-and-medium down pass-play actions to utilize in the effort to gain the required first-down yardage. Much like sprint-out passing, the quarterback's ability to run creates an extra (run) possibility for defensive pass coverage defenders to defend against. Furthermore, the addition of play-action faking and the counter action of the quarterback on bootlegs, naked bootlegs, and waggles make the quarterback's run/pass action all the more troubling for the defense, when the quarterback breaks back to the opposite side of the run-fake action.

Five-step timed, dropback pass action is another effective way to convert third-and-medium situations. In this scenario, however, the offense must be able to do a good job of protecting the quarterback versus a strong potential of defensive blitzes and line stunts. In that regard, the quarterback must be ready to release the five-step timed passes quickly, and the receivers must run crisp, quickly executed routes to help the quarterback in any tightly covered zone or man-to-man pass coverage action.

As a rule, screens can be very effective off of five-step timed dropback-pass actions, especially if the offensive coordinator has been calling such third-and-medium passes. The screens that might be most effective when faced with third-and-medium situations might very well be screens that come off of already utilized play-action passes, such as move/sprint-out-type passes and quick, three-step timed dropback passes, and five-step dropback passes. Diagram 14-5 offers an example of a third-and-medium play-call chart.

```
❏   Runs:

(10) Zoom Trey Rt 41 Trap              (10) Zoom Trey Lt 40 Trap
(11) Pistol Trey Rt 21 Read            (10) Pistol Trey Lt 20 Read
 (0) No-Backs Rt QB Draw                (0) No-Backs Lt QB Draw
(12) Doubles Rt Zin Zone Check         (12) Doubles Lt Zin Zone Check


❏   Passes:

(11) Gun Trey Rt 71 TB Delay           (11) Gun Trey Lt 71 TB Delay
(11) Zoom Trips Lt 90 Bench            (11) Zoom Trips Rt 90 Bench
(11) Soar Trey Rt 92                   (11) Soar Trey Lt 92
(10) Soar Gun Trey Rt 70 Flood         (10) Soar Gun Trey Lt 70 Flood
(11) Gun Deuce Lt 70 X-ray             (11) Gun Deuce Rt 70 X-ray
(10) Gun Deuce Rt Sprint Rt Dixie      (10) Gun Deuce Lt Sprint Lt Dixie
```

Diagram 14-5. An example of a third-and-medium play-call chart

Third-and-Medium-Long (Seven to Nine yards) Game Plan

A number of coaches classify third-and-long offense to be somewhere in the vicinity of third-and-seven, -eight, or -nine yards or greater. Over the course of my coaching career, I found that there can be a very useful third-down delineation that I refer to as third-and-medium/long (seven to nine yards) offense. This, specific, third-down yardage delineation helps to accommodate quickly thrown pass routes that, when executed, help to produce the needed seven to nine yards required to convert for a new set of downs. In reality, such pass routes, when completed, will produce positive passing yardage in the realm of 10 to 12 yards, easily converting third-down medium/long critical situations. As such, this third-down delineation takes an offense out of the classification of being "… manageable…," with the slightly increased, more stringent yardage gain needs.

In reality, the run game can still be effective in the third-and-medium/long down situations. Truth be known, with the possible exception of true run-option action, most runs have a tough time gaining seven to nine yards on the ground on such third-down situations. The best possibilities besides run-options are draws and quickly executed traps, utilized in efforts to burst forward north-south, through penetrating, pass-rushing defenders. Though truly a pass, shovel passes to running backs and tight ends are another viable course of action on third-and-medium/long situations.

More often than not, the quick, three-step timed passing game starts to run out of gas on the third-and-medium/long situations. As such, a quickly completed hitch or speed-out route that is tackled immediately may not gain needed first-down yardage. On the other hand, the exception is the slant route which, when completed with the receiver already streaking north-south, often provides the offense enough yardage to effectively convert a medium/long down situation.

Move/roll-out/sprint-out pass actions can also help to produce the needed third-and-medium/long gains. As such, move-actions help to disturb the rush lanes of the defensive fronts that, normally, may only have to rush quarterbacks who drop straight back to pass. In reality, however, the added amount of needed yardage can put a definite strain on the quarterback's ability to gain first-down yardage, if he has to run the football.

Misdirection passing (bootlegs, nakeds, and waggles) can definitely be effective in third-and-medium/long situations. Short, flat throws, however, can be somewhat limited in their ability to gain needed third-down yardage. The same factor is true when a quarterback is forced to run. Play-action passes lose a bit of their steam, since run fakes do not have as much validity, with the diminished likelihood of a run play being called.

In reality, dropback five-step and, possibly, seven-step dropback action provides the offensive coordinator with the best chance to being able to throw for third-and-medium/long down yardage. Most five-step timed passes (in the 10- to 12-yard range or more) should be able to get the yardage needed upon a completion. Underneath, crossing (dragging) routes can also be quite effective in these situations, since throwing to crossing receivers, while on the run, can often allow the running receiver to work upfield to gain the needed first-down yardage. This factor is extremely true, when working versus man-to-man coverage.

Screens should also have a definite place on the coordinator's play-call sheet on third-down-and-medium/long situations. As such, a pool of three to four screens gives the coordinator an ability to choose the screens he feels will be most effective versus a particular team's defense. This factor is especially true when the offense has a good passing game. Shovel passes are also extremely effective complementary pass-game concepts in the family of draws and screens. Diagram 14-6 provides an example of a third-and-medium/long play-call chart.

❏ Runs:

(10) Zoom Pistol Deuce Lt 50 Draw	(10) Zoom Pistol Deuce Rt 51 Draw
(10) Pistol Deuce Lt 20 Read	(10) Pistol Deuce Rt 21 Read

❏ Passes:

(10) Gun Trey Rt 92	(10) Gun Trey Lt 92
(10) Gun Deuce Lt Speed Screen Lt	(10) Gun Deuce Rt Speed Screen Rt
(11) Sink Gun Trey Rt 70 Y Follow	(11) Sink Gun Trey Lt 70 Y Follow
(11) Yac Gun Deuce Lt 70 Double Curls	(11) Yac Gun Deuce Rt 70 Double Curls
(10) Gun Deuce Lt 70 Verts	(10) Gun Deuce Rt 70 Verts
(11) Gun Trips Lt Load Sprint Rt Curl-X	(10) Gun Trips Rt Load Sprint Lt Curl-X
(11) Zoom Gun Deuce Lt Y Screen Lt	(11) Zoom Gun Deuce Rt Y Screen Rt

Diagram 14-6. An example of a third-and-medium/long play-call chart

Third-and-Long (10+ Yards) Game Plan

As much as an offensive coordinator would like to consistently be in either third-and-short (one to two yards) or manageable third-and-medium (three to six yards) down situations, when it is third down, in all likelihood, he will encounter a third-and-long (10+) situation in a game, much more often than he would prefer. When it's third-and-10 or longer, the advantage definitely shifts to the opposing defense.

Converting third-down situations is a tough enough chore without having to gain 10 or more yards. In such a circumstance, the defense doesn't have to, necessarily, force an incompletion. Short-to-intermediate routes can be completed, without the offense being able to convert needed yardage to gain a new first down. Defensive coverages can load up and align deeply to keep pass catching receivers from gaining the required deep yardage. The primary problem for the offensive coordinator, in this scenario, is to find ways to penetrate and defeat such prevent-type pass coverages.

A key consideration with regard to third-and-long situations is that the offensive coordinator must find ways to stretch and puncture such deep, prevent pass coverages with isolation and/or flood-type pass patterns. A well-prepared offensive coordinator chooses which of the third-and-long pass pattern plays from his pre-set, third-and-long package of plays that he feels will best attack a specific opponent's deep defending coverages during a game. Such an offensive coordinator must work hard to develop a successful third-and-long mentality with his offensive players and assistant coaches. He must be sure that those third-and-long pass patterns and offensive line pass protections are well-taught and well-practiced. A noteworthy goal for the offense is to statistically be the best third-and-long offense in its conference. Such a goal fits in well with an even bigger goal of being the best, overall, third-down team in the conference.

Trick plays can also be utilized on third-and-long situations, although the offensive coordinator must be careful regarding the type of trick plays being used. As such, the coordinator must realize that he will, almost assuredly, be facing some form of deep or prevent coverage. This factor is especially true, when the yardage need starts to grow to 20 yards of more. Long passes normally mean that the football will be in the air for a relatively significant amount of time, which can readily play into the hands of the defense's deep coverages and prevent coverage efforts.

There is one, solid, strategic consideration that can be effectively applied on what can be termed a third-and-long/long (20+ yards) situation. The underlying premise is to employ a quick-hitting draw/trap-type play or some form of screen or shovel pass to gain 10 or so yards in order to add to the ensuing fourth-down punt yardage. Diagram 14-7 provides an example of a third-and-long (10+ yards) play-call chart.

> ❏ Runs:
>
> | | |
> |---|---|
> | (10) Pistol Deuce Lt 41 Trap | (10) Pistol Deuce Rt 40 Trap |
> | (10) Zoom Deuce Lt 42 Read | (10) Zoom Deuce Rt 43 Read |
>
> ❏ Passes:
>
> | | |
> |---|---|
> | (10) Soar Gun Trey Rt Off Shovel | (10) Soar Gun Trey Lt Off Shovel |
> | (0) Yac Gun Trey Rt 70 Verts | (0) Yac Gun Trey Lt 70 Verts |
> | (11) Trips Lt Max 70 Double Post Wheel | (11) Trips Rt Max Double Post Wheel |
> | (10) Gun Trey Rt Scramble Rt | (10) Gun Trey Lt Scramble Lt |
> | (0) Nobs Lt 70 Verts X Drag | (0) Nobs Rt 70 Verts X Drag |

Diagram 14-7. An example of a third-and-long play-call chart

Pass Protection

On any pass play, a third-down pass or not, the total action of a pass play starts with the pass protection blocking efforts of the offense. If the pass protection blocking action is poor, the quarterback will, most likely, get sacked or be forced to scramble. When pressured, the quarterback will often be forced to throw off-balance, with, probably, poor passing fundamentals. On the other hand, he will be rushed in his attempt to execute his pass-delivery fundamentals.

Overall pass protection starts, first and foremost, with the offensive line. In addition to the quarterback and the offensive line, however, any of the offensive backs, tight ends, and wide receivers can be an intrinsic part of the overall success of an offense's pass protection package. In that regard, offensive backs and tight ends can provide sixth and seventh blockers to almost any pass blocking scheme. As such, an extra back or tight end could enable the use of a seven- or eight-man, maximum pass protection blocking scheme (end-of-line chip block releases can be a big part of maximum pass blocking thinking). All-in-all, the primary concern of employing such extra blockers is that the number of pass receivers shrinks as a result of the efforts to protect the quarterback.

Hot-route reads and sight-adjustment actions can be a big part of pass protection designs, given that such hot-route reads and sight adjustments can help to account for an, otherwise, unblocked defender. Hot-route reads are "go-to" pass routes that can actually be built into some of the pass patterns of the offense. As a result, a crossing route by a tight end can be thrown quickly, once an unblocked linebacker blitzes, which allows the quarterback to get his hot-route read route thrown, before he's hit by such a blitzing defender. Diagram 14-8 illustrates an example of a hot-route read pass to a vertical releasing tight end.

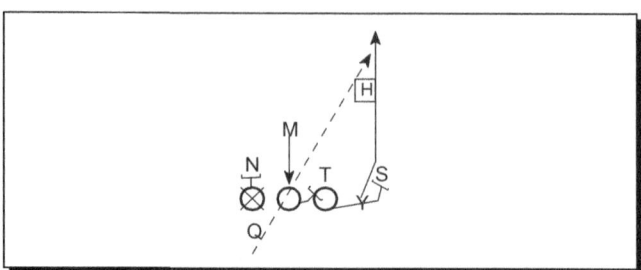

Diagram 14-8. (Y) tight end hot-route action

Sight-adjustment routes are short, quick adjustments of longer developing routes, as the quarterback adjusts his throw to quick-out, quick-hitch, or slant route-type passes. Such quickly thrown passes and pass completions are designed with the purpose of throwing the football before a specific, freed-up pass rusher can get to the quarterback to sack or pressure him. Diagram 14-9 provides an example of a sight-adjust route action by a slot back receiver versus a blitzing strong safety.

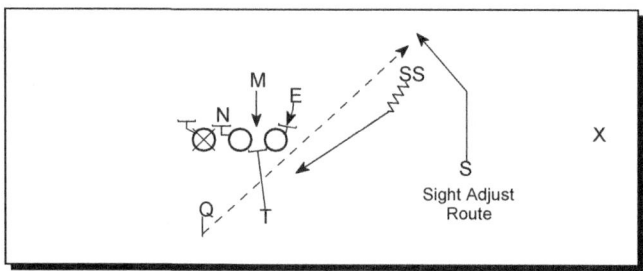

Diagram 14-9. Sight-adjust action versus a blitzing strong safety

The offensive coordinator should keep in mind that pass protection entails much more than the role of the offensive linemen. In reality, the offensive line can do an excellent job of blocking on a particular pass play, and the quarterback can still get pressured or sacked. More often than not, the reason for this situation can be because of poor blocking efforts and/or poor blocking fundamentals by a back or a tight end.

Pass blocking designs can start with dual-read protections tying into hot-read throws, if the two pass rushers assigned to the blocking back both rush. Utilizing a tight end for maximum protection can help give the quarterback the split second of extra time needed to get off a pass. Because pass protection is the start of all pass plays, the offensive coordinator must be certain that all aspects and facets of an offense's pass-blocking system is well-coordinated between the blockers, receivers, and quarterback.

Living or Dying by the Blitz

"Living or dying by the blitz ..." is an old football adage that has been utilized by coaches for many, many years. If a defense can get to the quarterback to put him under duress and/or sack him, the offense is in trouble. Quite simply, the offense must be able to handle blitz issues both through the pass-blocking system utilized and the execution of the fundamentals necessary to insure proper pass protection of the quarterback.

It is an offensive coordinator's role to make sure that the blitz can be handled by the offense's pass-protection system, as long as the individual blockers can properly execute their pass-protection techniques adequately. As a result, the offensive coordinator must be able to shift gears, if need be, at the drop of a hat, to help execute blitz control efforts to make the defense "... die by the blitz."

In reality, a number of offensive coordinators always have a separate game plan list of their "very best" anti-blitz plays and protections to be used, if a defense tried to surprise their offense with an unexpected blitz package. Diagram 14-10 details a game-ready, anti-blitz, emergency play call plan, if needed.

❐ Runs:
  • Inside zone
  • Outside zone with lead blocker
  • Trap
  • Lead/read option
  • Sweeps
  • QB sweep with extra lead back blocker

❐ Passes:
  • All three-step "passes" (hitches, slants, outs, and square-ins)
  • Swing screens, tight end and slot screens
  • Sprint-out passes (flat route blitz beaters)
  • Five-step dropback routes with crossing receivers (blitz beaters)
  • Five-step dropback passes with sight adjusts
  • Maximum protections

Diagram 14-10. An example of an anti-blitz, emergency, play call chart

Zone or Man-to-Man Execution

One extremely important concept that, unfortunately, is often overlooked is the factor of a pass route being executed differently versus zone and man-to-man coverages. Too often, coaches will have their quarterbacks, wide receivers, tight ends, and running backs execute passing and catching drills that are practiced versus zone-coverage techniques only. What happens when those receivers are faced with man-to-man coverage? Unfortunately, they usually meet with poor results.

When the coverage is zone coverage, a receiver should work/stem into the vacated zone holes of the total zone coverage and throttle down to hold such a vacated zone area into which the quarterback to throw his pass. If the coverage is man-to-man, the receiver should work to separate from the man-to-man coverage defender and then stay on the run at top speed to maintain such separation. Diagram 14-11 illustrates how a called quick pass game, six-yard, speed-out route versus zone coverage is adjusted to a quick pass game, five-yard, square-out route versus man-to-man coverage.

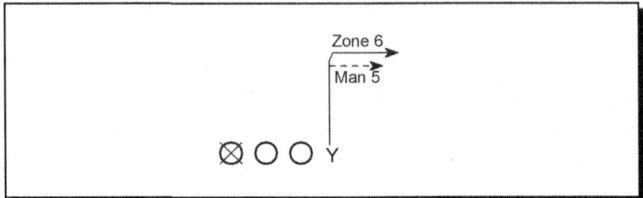

Diagram 14-11. An example of a zone, quick speed-out route adjusted to a man-to-man quick square-out route

CHAPTER 15
PLANNING THE RED ZONE OFFENSE

It's now Tuesday of a Friday night game week. As usual, Monday and Tuesday practices are heavy, fully geared practice days. The team's par (base) down offensive plan and its third-down offensive plan were developed yesterday, Monday. Today, Tuesday, is set aside for its red zone offensive plan and its goal line offensive plan. (Note: goal line planning will be discussed in Chapter 16.)

The concept of the red zone is directly tied into the goal line offensive concept. As can be seen, some coaches have deep red zone and black zone delineations that are really a part of their total red zone package. As such, Chapters 15 and 16 make up the close-knit red zone/goal line packaging that, along with par (base) down offense and third-down offense, are the four major concepts of game planning.

The Red Zone

The red zone, much like third-down offense, takes on its own, distinct characteristics. Yes, the offense is only 20 yards, or less, away from scoring a touchdown and 30, or less, yards away from kicking a possible field goal. The positive feature of being in the red zone for the offensive coordinator, who then utilizes his red zone offensive attack, is that he is in the red zone, closing in on the goal line in his effort to score a touchdown. On the other hand, the offensive coordinator must understand that there is a definite negative aspect of being in the red zone that can seriously affect his red zone attack plan.

The negative is the fact that the red zone offense must work in a shrunken-down, vertical distance as the coordinator closes in on the goal line and end zone. As such, he must be prepared to modify and/or adjust some of the pass routes in his passing arsenal to fit the limited amount of vertical distance he is afforded, if and when he attempts to pass the football into the end zone. In essence, the coordinator must be prepared for this factor, as the vertical distance of the field of play shrinks with each red zone yard the offense is able to gain toward the goal line.

Most coaches consider the start of the vertical aspect of the red zone to be the plus 20-yard line. As such, each gained offensive yard toward the goal line is a yard less of the vertical distance with which the red zone offense has to work. Gaining positive yardage in the red zone is a definite plus. On the other hand, what is affected by the limited vertical distance is the pass game in the red zone. What doesn't shrink for the red zone offensive attack and always stays consistent, no matter where the vertical position of the football is in the red zone, is the horizontal (lateral) distance of the field. As a result, the value of the offense attacking the 160 feet (53 1/3 yards) of horizontal distance can become an increasingly important aspect of a red zone offensive attack.

The opposing red zone defense is, certainly, put in a definite bind, as the offensive coordinator's red zone offense progresses closer and closer toward the goal line. On the other hand, as the opposing red zone defense is being backed up deep into the red zone by the positive advance of the coordinator's red zone offense, the defense's pass defensive efforts are assisted by being backed up to the lessened amount of vertical yardage that they have to pass cover.

The Deep Red Zone

Some offensive coordinators like to utilize what they call a deep red zone. The deep red zone is an area from the +21- to the +30-yard lines. The special "nature" of the deep red zone is a byproduct of the extra 10 total yards that are tacked on to the red zone. The vertical depth of the additional 10 yards of vertical distance helps the quarterbacks and receivers to be better able to execute deep-pass throws, rather than having to adjust passes in the shortened red zone and end zone area. Accordingly, the deep red zone can definitely help the quarterback, when he is throwing the football into the end zone from the expanded red zone. Diagram 15-1 offers an example of a deep red zone play call chart. It should be noted that only deep passes are shown as a part of the deep red zone, pass game planning.

❐   Passes:

(10) Soar Trey Rt Fake 24 Verts	(10) Pistol Trey Lt Fake 25 Verts
(11) Weak Trey Rt Max Dbl Post Wheel	(11) Weak Trey Lt Max Dbl Post Wheel
(12) Yac Wing Rt Toss Back QB Pass	(12) Yac Wing Lt Toss Back QB Pass

---

Diagram 15-1. An example of a deep red zone play call chart

Red Zone Game Planning

It is an unfortunate reality that references are often made about offenses that move up and down the field, but once they get to the red zone, they "…run out of gas!" There can be many reasons for this situation. A key reason can be the lack of an offensive coordinator adapting his team's pass game to the lack of vertical distance with which his team has to work in red zone situations. Another key reason might be the defense is "…bucking up," i.e., putting on the brakes on a long drive by the offense. Another possibility is that the defense, which rarely blitzes out in the field, may suddenly become a heavy blitz team in the red zone, in an effort to "…turn-up-the-heat" and attempt to apply heavy blitz pressure in hopes of "…turning-the-table" on the advancing red zone offense.

The bottom line for the offensive coordinator is to have his players "…bucked-up," as well, and aggressively work to put the football in the end zone or, at a minimum, kick a field goal. During the course of a football game, the offensive coordinator should be aware of the fact that his offense may not get that many red zone opportunities. As such, he needs to do all he can to be sure that his team cashes-in and scores as often as it can, every time it actually gets in the red zone.

Analyze an Opponent's Defensive Red Zone Tendencies

Analyzing an opponent's defensive red zone tendencies is a lot like analyzing an opponent's third-down tendencies. Similar to my efforts to analyze an opponent's third-down tendencies, I like to start by watching all of the successful plays (i.e., five+ yard runs and passes) executed by teams playing my opponent that have consistently been effective versus my opponent in the red zone. I look for successful play tendencies that are close, or similar, to runs and passes that are a part of my own offense.

As such, it is important for an offensive coordinator to know what makes a red zone defense tick. Is an opponent's the defense's red zone defense relatively the same or similar to its par (base) down defense? Does the red zone defense suddenly jump into a special red zone front? Does the opponent's red zone defense switch from zone pass coverages to man-to-man coverages or to a mixture of both? Does the red zone defense suddenly up its usage of blitzes and stunts? In reality, most defenses will stick to their base defense, with some change-of-pace attack concepts. What are those change-of-paces? What tendencies does the red zone defense show?

In the opposite vein, the offensive coordinator should analyze his team's own red zone offensive tendencies, because the opposition's defensive coordinator certainly will. Does his team use two favorite runs, when in the red zone, that have been hard for red zone defenses to stop over the course of the season?

Personally, I feel that the offensive coordinator should quickly test the red zone defense with his favorite, successful runs. If the run play works, run it again, spaced with other types of runs and passes in between. Perhaps the coordinator should vary the look for those favorite red zone run plays, with changes of personnel, formation, shifts, sets, and motions, so that the opponent's red zone defense doesn't get the run play looks it was expecting.

The offensive coordinator should utilize a similar strategy for his red zone pass game. As such, he should utilize his best pass game plays and disguise some, or all, of those pass plays with, again, personnel plans, formation changes, shifts, sets, and motions. The offensive coordinator must be sure, however, to utilize either the red zone pass game that fits the limited vertical distance of the red zone and end zone or use pass patterns or routes that, with slight modifications, can be successful in the red zone/end zone area.

Creating a Red Zone Run Game Plan

Ideally, an offensive coordinator's red zone run game offense is centered on run plays that are a part of his offense's par (base) down run offense. The reason for this factor is relatively straightforward—because an offense's par (base) down run game is, or should be, what the offense knows how to best execute. For the most part, the offensive coordinator should analyze from exchanged game videotapes what is the combination of the offense's best, most effective run plays and what he deems are the defense's red zone, run-game weaknesses.

If the offense's base run design is read-option football, and the offense has been consistently effective when running read-option action, the offensive coordinator should continue to invest in the read-option run game package in the red zone. Actually, that factor applies to any type of run or run-option action. Does the offensive coordinator believe he needs to make a personnel or formation change to help in the execution of the read-option run action? If he does, he should make such changes. Should a change be made in the read-option blocking scheme? If the offensive coordinator and/or offensive line coach believe they should, then they should. He should not run into a stone wall if he knows that the stone wall has a strong chance to stop his team. In other words, he should make needed alterations in his red zone run game, wherever necessary.

An offensive coordinator should willingly use his par (base) down offense to find his best red zone, run-game plays, whether they are quick hitting dives or zone runs, power run plays, sweeps and bellies, or run options. He should be sure to attack with his red zone offense, in a north-south manner, with no negative yardage plays. At that point, he should, then, ask himself what might be strong, supplemental, supporting run plays, such as counter or reverse action.

As such, an offensive coordinator should select his best run game plays to help him to attack what he believes are his opponent's weaknesses in the red zone. For example, given the recent advent of RPOs quick play-action passes (run/pass options) are an excellent alternative that ties directly into an offense's base, quick-hitting run game. Diagram 15-2 illustrates RPO (run/pass option) action, with a double speed-out route pattern.

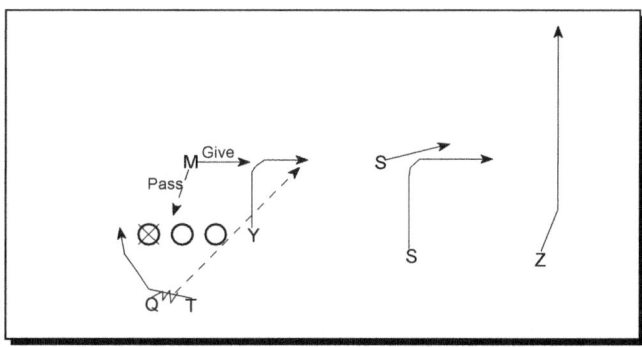

Diagram 15-2. RPO (run-pass option) action with double speed-out route pattern

Utilizing an Anti-Blitz Package

It is noteworthy that this section is not titled "red zone anti-blitz package." It just reads: anti-blitz package. When an offensive coordinator develops his anti-blitz package, it should encompass everything his team needs for stopping and/or for taking advantage of an opposing defense's blitz actions, especially in the red zone.

Regardless of whether an offensive coordinator sees, in his video analysis, that the opponent's red zone defense blitzes a lot or very little, he must be ready to handle a blitzing red zone defense. As noted previously, I always had a surprise plan on my play call sheet. Usually, it was a blitz pick-up package that I had ready for every game.

All-in-all, there's nothing worse than being surprised by a blitz package that the offensive coordinator didn't think was coming. Historically, the red zone has been the area on the football field where a normally non-blitzing defense has tried to surprise a red zone offense in an effort to "...make-something-happen." Accordingly, the offensive coordinator must make sure that the offense is ready to pick up the blitz threats, no matter where the offense is on the field or what quarter of the game it is.

In reality, failures in the red zone are often devastating. A chance to catch up, tie a game, or go ahead is often determined by success or a lack thereof in the red zone. As noted previously, since visits to the red zone are often limited in a game, the offensive coordinator needs to be certain to cash in on them, whenever he can.

Worry About Pass Protection First for the Red Zone Pass Game

Creating a red zone pass game plan must start with consideration for anti-blitz protection. In reality, an opposing defense may not blitz at all during the course of a game, until it is pushed back into the red zone. Quite often, a defensive coordinator will feel the pressure of the goal line inching up from the rear.

Whether an opposing red zone defense blitzes or not, the offensive coordinator must be sure that his anti-blitz package is ready to perform effectively, right from the minute that his offense enters the red zone. In that regard, as has already been discussed, an offensive coordinator must have a well-taught and well-executed anti-blitz plan, or package, ready to be put into play. This factor is especially true, when his offense begins to enter the opposing team's red zone.

One valid reason to like the quick, three-step timed, dropback pass action in the red zone is that the quick pass game is blitz control. Having the quarterback getting the football away quickly on a pass greatly affects the defense's chance to get to a quarterback to pressure or sack him. Furthermore, defending quick pass routes is difficult, due to the fact that the distance of the routes is relatively short, as well as their quickly timed execution. Hitches, with their ability to fade-route adjust versus squatted or pressed man-to-man coverage, are blitz-beater routes, as are speed-outs and slant routes. Other than fade-route adjustments for hitches, quick-pass routes need little, if any, route running adjustments. Actions, such as hot routes and sight adjustments, are, normally, utilized by deeper routes and pass patterns.

An offensive coordinator can certainly make quick adjustments at the beginning of the week in an effort to get an anti-blitz package ready for a specific opponent. On the other hand, an anti-blitz package works best, when it is inserted into the total design of a passing game and its related pass protection concepts early in the pre-season. On a tight end cross/drag route that works quickly across a formation, the crossing receiver needs to understand that he must look up quickly for a possible hot throw over the middle, if both the quarterback and the crossing receiver see the inside linebacker, or linebackers, blitz in front of the crossing-route receiver. In this fashion, an anti-blitz action is built into the pass pattern. An example of an inside-crossing route, anti-blitz, hot route action is shown in Diagram 15-3.

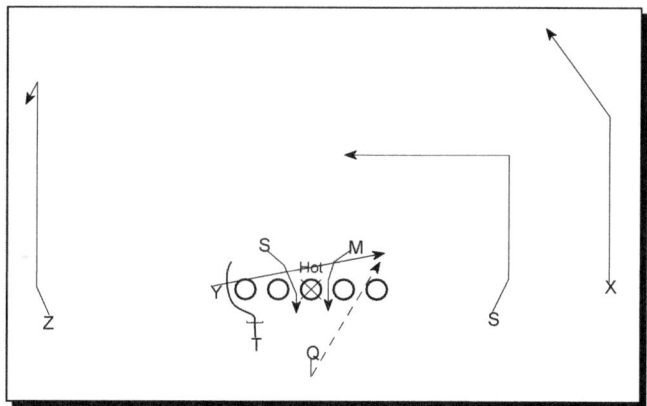

Diagram 15-3. An example of hot route passing to a crossing/drag route

Sight-adjusting is a common blitz-beater action, used when a secondary defender blitzes through the core or off the edge of an offensive formation. When sight-adjusting, wide receivers are assigned to read safety/cornerback defenders prior to and during the snap of the football. This step is undertaken for possible secondary-blitz reads. Slants, or fast-developing, on-the-line-of-scrimmage, one-step hook-up routes can preempt the basic routes of a pass pattern called either in the huddle or while on the line of scrimmage. Diagram 15-4 illustrates the use of sight adjusting a split-end side to help control/attack a secondary cornerback blitz.

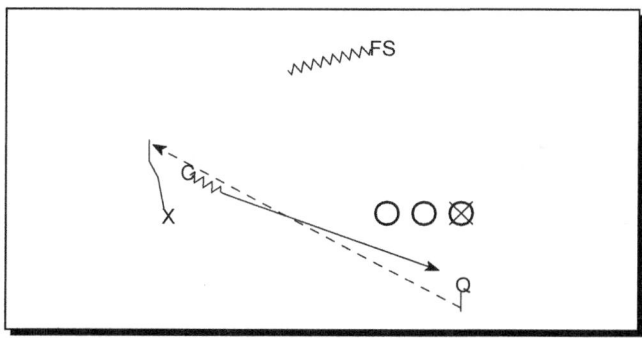

Diagram 15-4. Sight-adjusting to control a secondary cornerback blitz

RPO (run/pass options) action helps to hold and/or control linebackers, as well as strong safeties/outside linebackers, from filling, or blitzing, assigned run lanes along the line of scrimmage or off the outside edge of an offensive front. Most RPOs are not actually considered blitz-beater actions. When isolated, however, assigned defenders can be sucked up into the line of scrimmage with run fakes, producing vacated lanes into which the quarterback can pass. Diagram 15-5 shows the use of RPO (run/pass options) to help isolate and control inside and outside linebacker types and, possibly, strong safeties, to clearly present run or pass reads.

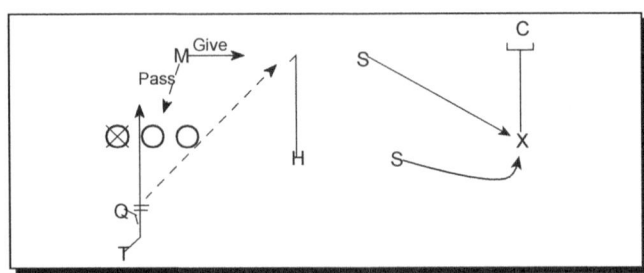

Diagram 15-5. Using an RPO (run/pass option action)
to control a linebacker

Maximum protections with seven, and even eight, protectors can, and should, be an excellent means of allowing for longer pass patterns to develop—and don't forget end-of-line chip blocking possibilities. Play-action faking, with a maximum protection, backside tight end blocking and a faking running back's linebacker check/block assignment is illustrated in Diagram 15-6.

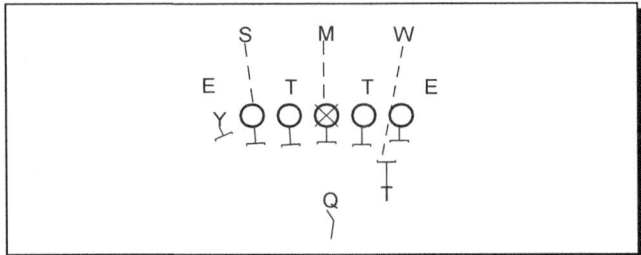

Diagram 15-6. An example of a maximum, seven-man,
pass block protection

Creating a Red Zone Pass Game Plan

When creating a red zone passing plan, the offensive coordinator should, once again, carefully study the red zone computer analysis of the opponent to determine what passes have been shown to be effective in attacking that opponent in the red zone with the pass game. Another possibility would be for the offensive coordinator to have his team's red zone assistant coach specialist comb and study the analysis to help identify successful pass plays against the opponent's red zone defense. Studying such successful pass plays can help the coordinator or assistant coach red zone specialist to ascertain which of those successful red zone passes are similar, by design, to existing offensive plays to possibly be chosen to be part of their team's red zone pass game plan.

Given that the strong threat of the blitz game in the red zone has already been reviewed, the quick, three-step timed pass game is an excellent countermeasure in that situation. The major reason for employing the red zone, quick-pass game action in this scenario is (as has been already been discussed) that it is an excellent blitz-beater package. As such, quick-pass game hitches and quick-outs, when completed, can result in six- to seven-yard (or more) gains. Slants, of course, have the capacity of an even greater amount of gained yardage, given the ability of the receiver to catch on the run and efficiently burst upfield.

Hitch-go and slant-go routes are excellent red zone pass game alternatives, as are fade adjustments for hitch routes versus squatted, or press man, coverage. In addition, it is essential for the offensive coordinator to emphasize to his quick-pass game receivers that they need to be ready to make man-to-man adjustments, when necessary.

Along with quick-pass game passing, RPOs (run/pass options) are excellent run-pass concepts that can be utilized in the red zone. This factor is especially true when the runs have quick hitting, north/south designs that can help to prevent negative yardage. Furthermore, RPOs' usage of quickly thrown tight end/slot back vertical routes, speed-outs, hitches, and slants helps create an extremely effective red zone run/pass option package.

Another effective alternative in the red zone are sprint out-action passes. As such, by attacking one side of the defense or the other, the backside of the defense is limited in its efforts to pressure the quarterback on his sprint-out run action. Furthermore, with the quarterback downhill-attacking the line of scrimmage, his running threat becomes an extra offensive threat for the pass defense to defend.

Quickly thrown, five-step drop passes can also be extremely effective in the red zone pass attack. The coordinator just needs to be sure that the routes the quarterback is working/throwing to can effectively fit into the shrunken, vertical distance of the red zone, as it stretches toward the backend line. In addition, quickly thrown five-step drop pop-up-and-throw passing action can also be extremely effective, as long as the quarterback sticks to the timing of that passing action and is not slow on his pass-release delivery.

As such, a slow, delayed seven-step timing pass-action has limited usage in the red zone. Whatever the pass package is for the offensive coordinator's red zone attack, he must be sure to utilize quickly timed passes to help defeat a defense's blitz efforts, unless the offense is using maximum pass protections.

If the red zone defense uses a significant amount of man-to-man coverage for a heavy blitz threat, the offense's red zone pass package should focus on employing crossing routes and isolation routes. Diagram 15-7 illustrates crossing-route action to attack man-to-man coverages.

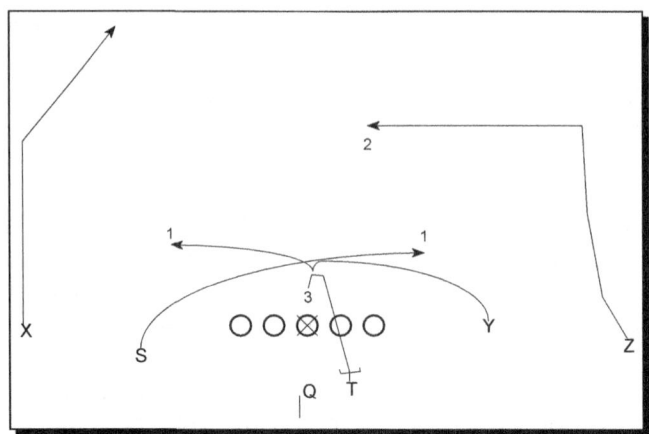

Diagram 15-7. Crossing-route action to attack man-to-man coverage

Diagram 15-8 details the use of one-on-one isolation, option routes to attack man-to-man Coverage. (Note that the option routes are built to attack both zone and man-to-man coverages.)

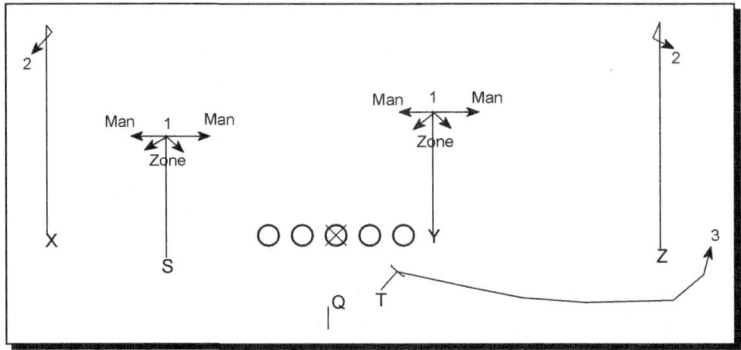

Diagram 15-8. One-on-one isolation option routes to attack man-to-man coverage

Zone coverage pass attacks are, normally, designed to create two-on-one or three-on-two, overloaded flood-type coverages. Diagram 15-9 shows a lateral (side-by-side) two-on-one curl/flat route concept, in which both receivers try to effectively work into side-by-side, vacated zone passing holes.

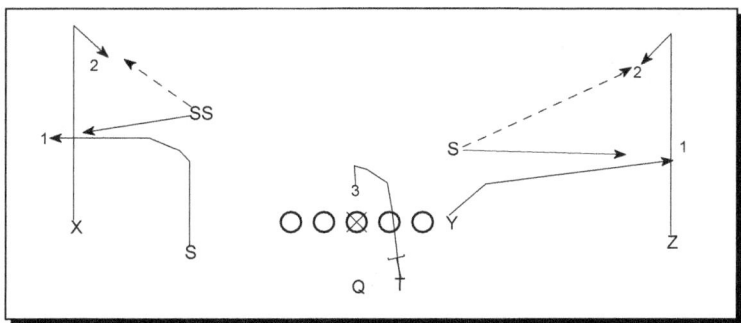

Diagram 15-9. Lateral (side-by-side) two-on-one curl/flat zone route concept

Diagram 15-10 illustrates a vertical, high-to-low, flood-route pattern concept, in which the quarterback reads the high streak route down to the flood route and then down to the flat route. The flat route is, however, the blitz beater route to be used versus blitz pressure issues. The offensive coordinator should be careful to make sure he has enough vertical distance in which the streak route is able to work. If the streak route runs out of vertical distance, the receiver should break flat to the inside, once he realizes he is on top of the end line in the end zone.

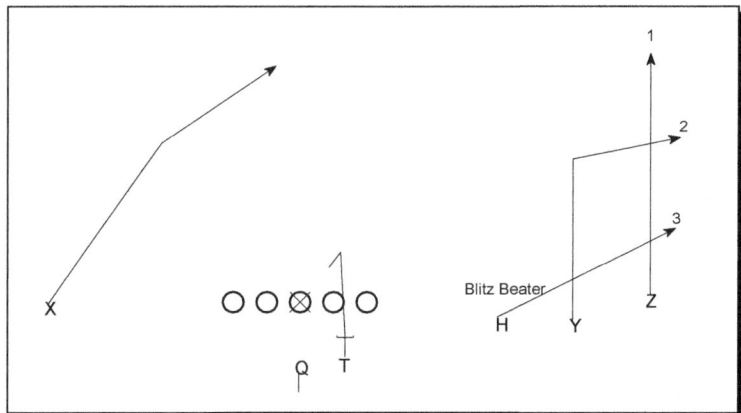

Diagram 15-10. Vertical, high-to-low flood route concept

The final red zone route/pattern concept to be considered is the possible need for route modification to fit the possible shrunken vertical distance of the red zone. Out on the field, with no major concerns for vertical distance considerations, the delineation for a post-corner route would be to push the top of the route (the corner aspect) to 30 yards from the line of scrimmage toward the sideline. On the other hand, if the line of scrimmage is on the 15-yard line in the red zone, the post-corner route would have to modify/adjust the 30-yard distance to 25 yards from the line of scrimmage to the back corner end line flag. This shortening/modification of a post-corner route action from the 15- and 10-yard line of the red zone to the back corner, end line corner flag is detailed in Diagram 15-11.

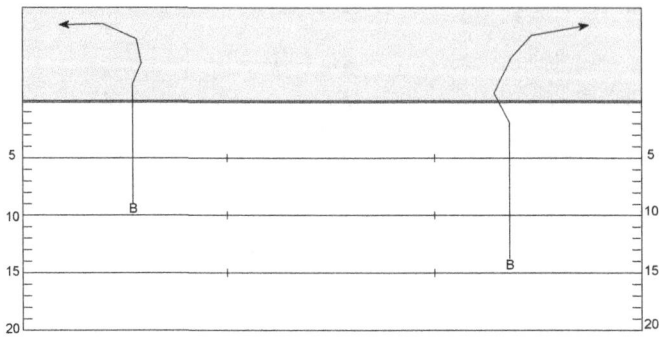

Diagram 15-11. Adjusted shortening modification of a post-corner route in the red zone

Diagram 15-12 provides an example of a red zone play call chart.

❏   Runs:

(12) Strong Whip Wing Lt 35 Power   (12) Strong Whip Wing Rt 36 Power
(10) Zoom Deuce Lt 41 Trap   (10) Zoom Deuce Rt 40 Trap
(11) Weak Deuce Lt 20 Read   (11) Weak Deuce Rt 21 Read
(12) Doubles Rt Over Zone Check   (11) Doubles Lt Over Zone Check
(13) Wac Wing Rt Tite 48   (13) Wac Wing Lt Tite 49

❏   Passes:

(12) Wing Lt Twins Whip 90 Slant   (12) Wing Rt Twins Whip 90 Slant
(11) Trey Rt Off 90 Bench and Up   (11) Trey Lt Off 90 Bench and Up
(12) Wac Dbls Rt Act 24 Max Streaks   (12) Wac Dbls Lt Act 25 Max Streaks
(11) Zoom Gun Deuce Lt 70 Verts   (11) Zoom Gun Deuce Rt 70 Verts
(12) Weak Dbls Rt Act 24 P.C.s   (12) Weak Dbls Lt Act 25 P.C.s
(11) Soar Deuce Lt 25 Naked   (11) Soar Deuce Rt 24 Naked

Diagram 15-12. An example of a sample red zone play call chart

The Black Zone

The black zone is a specific area at the bottom of the red zone that is inside the +10-yard line, a situation in which the offense cannot get a first down. Actually, the black zone extends toward the goal line to a point where the goal line offense starts. This zone of the field is mainly used for specially designated pass patterns and pass routes employed in this limited amount of vertical yardage distance in which to work. Having a specific black zone designation can help a lot, particularly when game planning to defeat special coverages such as a seven-across zone coverage, into which it can be difficult to pass the football. Diagram 15-13 highlights a high/low, tight end/running back read from the seven-yard line in the black zone.

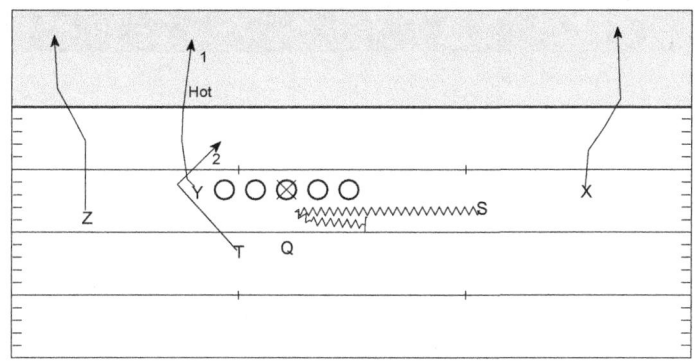

Diagram 15-13. Black zone, high/low, tight end/running back pattern concept

Diagram 15-14 details an example of a black zone play call chart.

❐ Runs:

(12) Wing Lt 35 Power Check 92	(12) Wing Rt 36 Power Check 92
(12) Whip Wing Strong Lt 49 QB	(12) Whip Wing Strong Rt 48 QB
(11) Fly Trips Lt 28 Sweep	(11) Fly Trips Rt 29 Sweep

❐ Passes:

(11) Wac Bunch Rt Sprint Rt China	(11) Wac Bunch Lt Sprint Lt China
(10) Deuce Rt Empty Texas Chair	(10) Deuce Lt Empty Texas Chair
(11) Zoom Bunch Rt 70 Y Follow	(11) Zoom Bunch Lt 70 Y Follow
(0) Lt Empty Fly Sprint Rt Jet	(0) Rt Empty Fly Sprint Lt Jet

Diagram 15-14. An example of a black zone play call chart

CHAPTER 16
PLANNING THE GOAL LINE OFFENSE

Along with par (base) down offense, third-down offense, and red zone offense, goal line offense is the last of the "big four" major game planning concepts. These four concepts should be intently studied and analyzed to create four major run- and pass-game plans. Once again, the lack of vertical distance from the start of the goal line offensive yardage area (plus-four or plus-three) to the back end line of the end zone is one of the major issues concerning goal line passing offense. The other major concern of goal line offense is the often major change undertaken to heavy personnel offensive fronts to contend with beefed up defensive goal line fronts, such as the 6-2, 6-5, and the bear-46 (double eagle) goal line defenses, in an effort to shut down goal line run games.

Goal Line/End Line Delineations

The end zone starts with the goal line. Once any part the carried football, in possession of an offensive player, crosses the front (fieldside) edge of the goal line, a touchdown is scored. Accordingly, the goal line is the most frontal part of the end zone. The end zone area is encased by the sidelines and the end line, which, when physically encroached (e.g., footstep) results in being out of bounds.

The actual field-of-play yardage delineations for what is termed goal line offense depends greatly on the style of play applied by the offense and the defense in the short-yardage area directly in front of the goal line. As a result, goal line offenses and defenses can start their goal line attack anywhere from the one- to the four-yard line.

As a rule, goal line offense is perceived as being more in the one- to three-yard range. Although it certainly is possible, a goal line offense could also start at the five-yard line, but rarely does so.

Until fairly recently, goal line offenses and defenses were consistently determined by the sudden additions of beefed-up, heavy personnel (e.g., extra tight ends, fullbacks, and, at times, offensive linemen on offense and extra defensive linemen, linebackers, and safeties on defense). More often than not, such goal line personnel and formational adjustments are initially made by the offense, followed by defensive substitutions and formation changes to match-up with the offense.

With the latest trend of spread and/or read-option offensive football, many offenses have discontinued switching to such beefed-up, heavy personnel variation changes. Instead, they, simply, have continued using much of their par (base) down offensive attack all the way to the goal line, relying heavily on run-option and outside, sweep-type run plays, as well as out-flanking, laterally designed pass patterns.

A major reason for the success of run-option and sweep action on the goal line is the factor that goal line offenses are never limited horizontally from sideline to sideline. This aspect, certainly, is not true for goal line passing offenses, although they still have the same horizontal width of the field that the run game does. Goal line passing actions, however, are definitely limited by the amount of vertical yardage with which the goal line/end zone offense has to work.

Analyze the Opponent's Goal Line Tendencies

Analyzing an opponent's goal line defensive tendencies is a lot like analyzing an opponent's par (base) down tendencies, their third-down tendencies, and their red zone tendencies. Just as in the efforts to analyze all of those game-situational tendencies, the offensive coordinator can start the process by watching and analyzing all of the successful plays that have been effective versus an opponent in the goal line zone area. The offensive coordinator can look for successful goal line play tendencies that are close, or similar, to runs and passes that are a part of his own goal line offensive philosophy. While watching for those successful run and pass plays, the coordinator is able to discern the type of goal line defensive front and coverages he, in all probability, will soon be facing.

Personally, I believe in the same multiple personnel and formational approach that I adhere to for par (base) downs, third downs, and red zone downs that I do for goal line offense. In reality, the offensive coordinator should want to know what the structure of the goal line defense is that he is going to face. Will it be a 6-2 goal line front, a 6-5 goal line defense, a double eagle, 46 defense? Or, will the defense remain in his base offense, with some modifications? Does the opponent's goal line defense use zone coverage? Man-to-man coverage? Or, does the goal line defense's coverage switch back and forth from zone to man-to-man or man-to-man to zone? Does the opposition's goal line defense suddenly up the usage of its blitzes and stunts? Will the opposition's defense stick to one main goal line defensive front? Or, will the opposition's goal line front jump around to produce a mixture of varied goal line looks?

From the opposite side of the football, the offensive coordinator should also analyze his team's own goal line offensive tendencies. Does his goal line offense base itself on a dive, dive-option series with a sweep, an isolation blast run play, and a counter run play? Which of those goal line run plays seem to be consistently effective—the one's the offensive coordinator will think of as his "…bread and butter…" goal line offensive plays. Does the coordinator have two favorite runs, when on the goal line, that have been difficult for goal line defenses to stop?

In reality, once a goal line situation arises, the offensive coordinator should quickly test the opposition's goal line defense with his favorite, most successful goal line run and pass plays. Subsequently, if those preferred goal line run plays seem to be bogging down, the coordinator should vary the personnel and formational looks for those goal line runs and pass plays in an effort to throw off the focus of the defense.

When utilizing his goal line pass game, the offensive coordinator should approach the goal line passing game in a similar way he does for the goal line run game. In other words, the coordinator should use his best goal line pass game plays and disguise some, or all, of those pass plays with personnel plans, formation changes, shifts, sets, and motions.

The major issue facing the offensive coordinator is that he must be sure to utilize the goal line pass game pattern principals and routes that fit the limited vertical distance of the end zone, i.e., 10 vertical yards. As such, if the pass patterns and routes of the goal line passing design don't fit the end zone area, the offensive coordinator must utilize pass patterns or routes that, with slight modifications, can be successful in the goal line, end zone area.

As was alluded to a number of times in Chapter 15, red zone offenses and goal line offenses are often "…joined at the hips…," with regard to their importance to one another. Much of that importance deals with the concept of the football field shrinking vertically, as the offense closes in on the goal line and the end zone. In fact, closing in on and getting over the goal line and into the end zone is the major goal of both red zone and goal line run/pass offenses.

Creating a Goal Line Run Game Plan

As before, an offensive coordinator is strongly encouraged to start out, when he's attempting to put together his goal line run-game package, by looking to his par (base) down run offense. He should begin by examining what he feels are his best, most efficient par (base) down run plays and see if they can be applicable in helping to produce an effective goal line ground game. At times, an effective par (base) down run play can be extremely effective out on the field, but struggle when faced with attacking goal line defenses. In reality, such run plays should be discarded from a coordinator's goal line attack package, unless some type of adjustments can be made to make them goal-line effective.

Quick-hitting run plays (e.g., dives, bellies, zone runs, etc.) help to explosively crease goal line defensive fronts. What an offensive coordinator must realize is that slipping through a crack via the blocking of the offensive line, tight ends, and blocking backs might be all that is needed for the short yard, or two, to score a touchdown, or, to gain a few yards to help put the goal line offense that much closer to scoring with the remaining downs.

Power goal line running is an excellent way to help get the football over the goal line. As such, the isolation/blast play can produce a maximum amount of blocking fire power, with extra linemen, tight ends, and blocking backs to help get the football over the goal line. In reality, an isolation/blast jump play is, often, an effective way to catapult a ballcarrying running back over the top of a pile of stacked up defensive linemen and linebackers. Power run plays, with pulling linemen and kick-out blocks, are also an extremely effective way to successfully pound the football into the end zone.

Sweeps, be they tailback/offset-back sweeps, quarterback sweeps, or fly sweeps, can help to stretch defensive-front defenders along the line of scrimmage in order to create run-lane creases for the ballcarriers. Run-option plays of all kinds (e.g., double- and triple-options) can also be extremely effective for both inside and outside run/option play facets. Furthermore, spread offenses and read-option offenses of all kinds can help to thin out defenses to create run creases for the short distance, goal line run-play needs.

Special goal line run plays that are not a part of an offense's par (base) down offense are often used by goal line offenses to help gain tactical goal line advantages. For example, a power I set, with two extra big offensive linemen in the backfield in front of a tailback, can be an extremely effective way to "…road-grade…" a run path into the end zone. The only major problem that can evolve as a result of using such special goal line plays is that they must be coached consistently and thoroughly to make sure they are truly ready to use come game time. In that regard, the offensive coordinator must be sure that such "special" plays will not unravel to the point of being a failure a yard or two away from scoring a touchdown.

Working the End Zone With the Pass Game

Once an offense gets into the goal line offensive area (plus-four to goal line), the offensive coordinator must have a goal line pass package that is specially fitted, or shaped, to the limited, vertical yardage of the goal line area (plus-four yards to the goal line) and the end zone (plus-10 yards of vertical area from the goal line to the end line). In reality, 11 to 14 yards of vertical area is not a lot of room in which to work a pass pattern, especially when the end zone, itself, only gives the goal line offense 10 vertical yards in which to function.

Accordingly, when executing pass routes into the end zone, receivers must understand how to fit routes and pass patterns into the parameter constraints of the end zone (horizontally, 160 feet of width, and vertically, 10 yards of end zone depth). Diagram 16-1 details the distance parameters of the end zone, with six, short, 18-inch vertical markers to indicate the four corners of the rectangular end zone, plus the two vertical markers on the end line that indicate the positioning of the field hash marks.

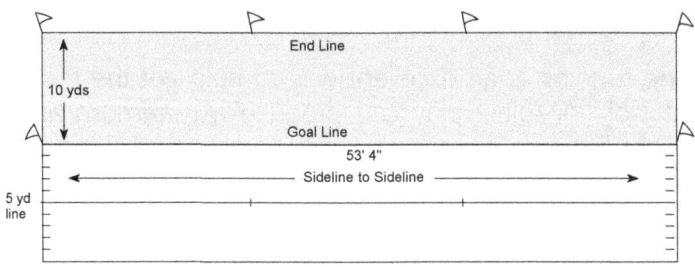

Diagram 16-1. The distance parameters of the end zone

The major issue that an offensive coordinator has to address with regard to goal line/end zone passing is the vertical-yardage snugness of the end zone. Because there are only 10 yards of vertical yardage from the goal line to the end line in which receivers can work, there are some key passing concepts that should be kept in mind, when attacking goal line defenses and the end zone.

The first key goal line/end zone concept is for any short-depth route, with a deeper route working behind it, to adjust the short route to one yard over/past the goal line. For example, if an offense's flat route is normally run three yards deep, and the line of scrimmage is three yards deep, the flat receiver should deepen his route slightly to four yards deep, which is one yard over the goal line. Why? The major reason, and an important one at that, is that when the flat route is run one yard over/past the goal line, a catch automatically produces a touchdown. On the other hand, if the same receiver ran his normal, three-yard flat route directly over the goal line, he might reach back and catch the football before the goal line. If he is immediately tackled, there is a good chance that the receiver will not be able to get the football to the goal line, thereby preventing him from scoring a touchdown.

A second reason for adjusting the course of a short-pass route to be run only one yard over the goal line is to help a deep-receiver route to produce a high/low relationship with the adjusted, one-yard-over-the-goal-line route of the underneath, flat route receiver. The deeper, end line pass-route receiver must work his pass route one yard from the end zone's end line. This step is undertaken on high/low-read end zone pass patterns to help produce a maximum distance of eight yards of separation from the front and back end zone receiver routes. Such separation helps to prevent one defender from being able to cover both the high and the low receiver routes. Diagram 16-2 illustrates proper high/low vertical route displacement of two receivers in the end zone.

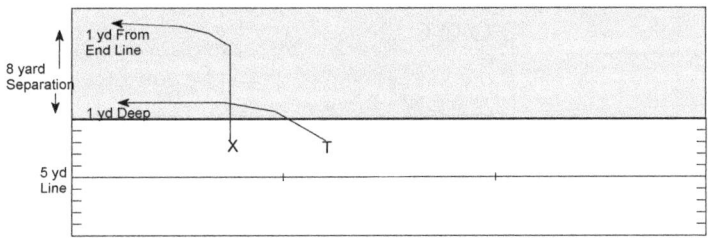

Diagram 16-2. Proper high/low end zone vertical route displacement

End Zone Pass Patterns Must Not Be Cluttered

The offensive coordinator must be sure that he utilizes, or adapts, pass patterns that are not cluttered when passing into the end zone. Improper route running by receivers at improper depths can easily produce such route-pattern clutter. Diagram 16-3 demonstrates how a goal line pattern can easily become cluttered by, simply, trying to run a flood pass pattern into an area that, by design, cannot properly space all three of the flood pattern receivers. The outside deep streak route receiver quickly runs out of room, in his effort to clear out the space to be worked by the flood route receiver. Even if the streak receiver breaks-off his streak route and squares his route to the inside, directly in front of the end line (as shown in Diagram 16-3), there still will be inadequate spacing of the three receivers in the overall flood pass pattern design. The flood pass pattern will, simply, just be too cluttered.

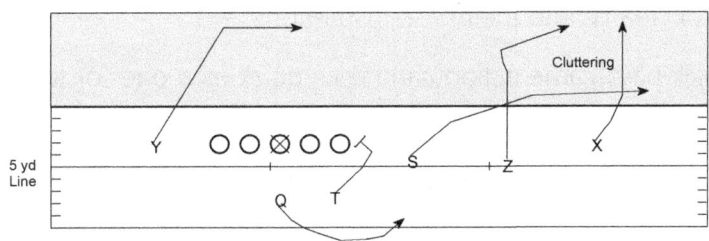

Diagram 16-3. End zone flood pass pattern cluttering

What can be done to clear up such a cluttering of routes in the flood pass pattern shown in Diagram 16-3? One answer is to eliminate the widest receiver from the pass pattern. The widest receiver can, simply, motion across the formation to help thin out both the flood pass pattern and, possibly, the goal line pass coverage. In reality, man-to-man coverage should, actually, pull out the coverage of a man-to-man coverage defender covering the motion receiver, as shown in Diagram 16-4.

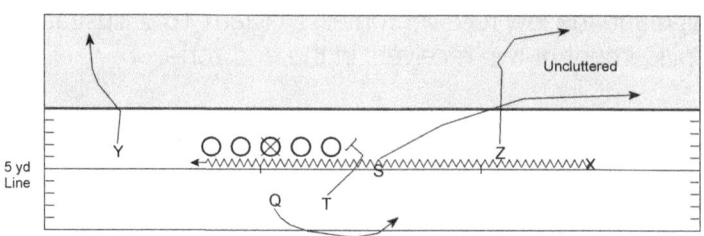

Diagram 16-4. Using motion to unclutter a pass pattern

Creating a Goal Line Pass Game Plan

After the aforementioned of what is actually the goal line area, the end zone, and working the end zone with the limited amount of vertical yardage distance, the next step is to identify and review pass patterns, pass routes, and modes of passing attacks that can help the offense to score touchdowns through the air.

Initially, the use of quick-passing actions should come to the forefront of any goal line passing attack. Since both the offense and the opposing defense are working in a tight, condensed area of 14 yards or less of vertical football field yardage, the overall action of the goal line offense and the opposing goal line defense tends to be fast and furious. As a result, the quick, three-step timed passing game is a good place to start, when creating a goal line pass-game plan.

In the quick passing game, the offensive line has the advantage of being able to aggressively attempt to negate the rush of the defensive front, since they can take the rush on quickly and powerfully, not having to drop back off the line of scrimmage in their pass sets. As such, the offensive linemen are able to strongly punch their blocks into pass-rushing defenders at, or near, the line of scrimmage, before the defenders can get a "head of steam" into their pass-rush efforts.

In reality, quick pass-game action can be as quick as a one- or two-stepped timed throw, when the offense starts out with fade route-type execution. On a fade route, the ball is thrown toward the end line corner flag on the sideline, two to three yards from the end line. Attached to fade-route execution is the fade back-shoulder throw possibility, when a covering cornerback is positioned on top of the fade receiver. The fade route and a fade route back-shoulder throw action are illustrated in Diagram 16-5.

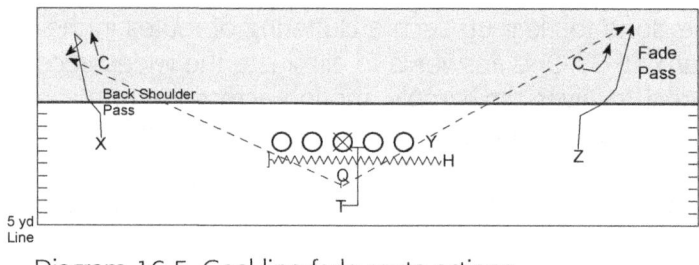

Diagram 16-5. Goal line fade route actions

Diagram 16-6 shows a fade/comeback route, in which the fade route receiver fakes the fade route to, approximately, six to seven yards deep in the end zone. Subsequently, the fade route receiver looks back to the inside, off of his inside foot plant, to fake looking for a fade ball throw and then abruptly turns to the outside to drive back to the front corner flag for a low, driving throw from the quarterback. Quick three-step timed dropback pass action or sprint-out action can both effectively enact a fade/comeback throw (Diagram 16-6). The sprint-out action adds the dimension of the possibility of the quarterback running into the end zone for a touchdown.

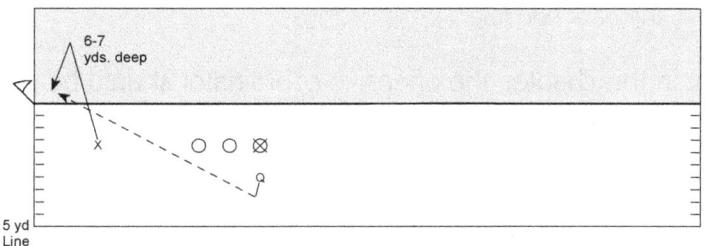

Diagram 16-6. Goal line fade/comeback route

Slant and quick-out routes are excellent quick pass-game routes to utilize on the goal line versus both man-to-man or zone coverages. Diagram 16-7 shows slant and slant-go action on the left side of the diagram and quick-speed out/flat action on the right side of the diagram. On these double-route concepts, the quarterback works to the least covered side.

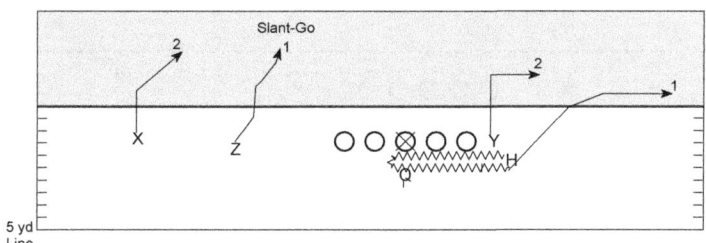

Diagram 16-7. Goal line double-slant/speed-out route
pattern combination

Diagram 16-8 illustrates a double square-in route pattern, with a flattened, over-the-top, post-corner route, working the back end line, away from the underneath square-in routes. The "Z and the "X" work one to two yards deep into the end zone and square-in, quickly looking to work into a voided zone hole or staying on the move versus man-to-man coverage. The "S" slotback's post-corner works the back end line, and either looks for a voided zone hole by the coverage or stays on the run versus man-to-man coverage.

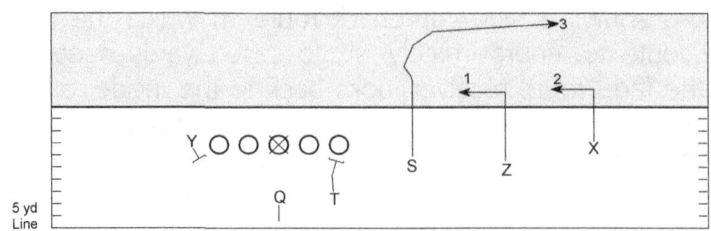

Diagram 16-8. Double square-in goal line route pattern with an over-the-top, bending post-corner route, working the back end line

At this point in this chapter, the offensive coordinator should be getting a good feel for the need for isolation, one-on-one routes in the end zone in the vertically shortened end zone area. This awareness goes along well with the need for quick, three-step timed drop quarterback passing.

Diagram 16-9 details a Z follow goal line pass pattern from a bunch formation to create a three-receiver quarterback scan from left to right, in what is popularly known as a triangle read concept. The Z follow pass pattern is an excellent pattern to attack both zone and man-to-man goal line pass coverages. The quarterback's pass timing is slightly lengthened to a quick, five-step dropback pass action to allow for his scanning-read action.

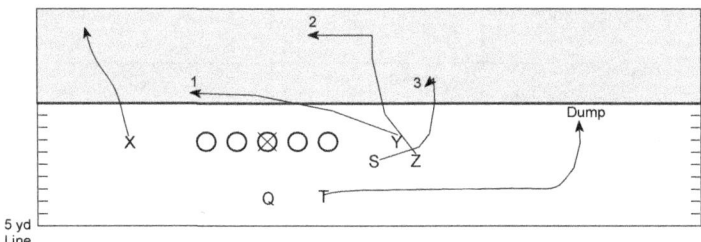

Diagram 16-9. Z follow goal line pass pattern to attack both zone and man-to-man coverages

Versus the heavy use of man-to-man coverage on the goal line by the defense, crossing-type routes are also an excellent means of attacking such man-to-man coverages. Diagram 16-10 illustrates a three-receiver crossing action off of a goal line, sprint-out pass action.

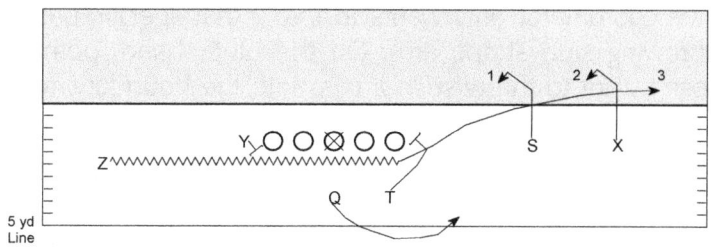

Diagram 16-10. Goal line sprint-out crossing pass
pattern to attack man-to-man coverages

Diagram 16-11 points out the more delayed five-step timed drop quarterback goal line-throw crossing action versus man-to-man coverage, which is equally as good versus zone coverage. As was previously noted, Diagram 16-12 shows flood pass action out of a bunch set, which is good for attacking both zone and man-to-man goal line pass coverages.

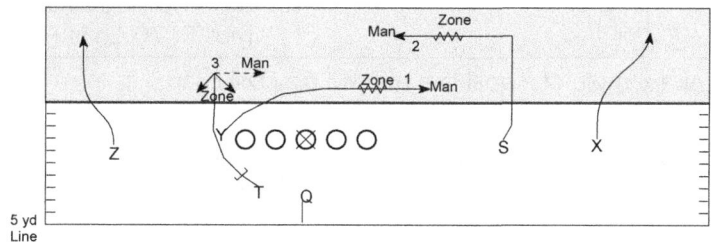

Diagram 16-11. Five-step drop timed crossing action to
attack both man-to-man and zone coverages

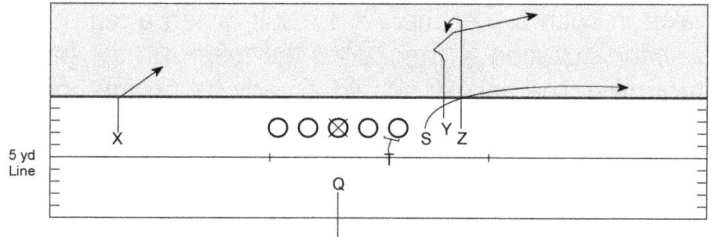

Diagram 16-12. Flood pass pattern to attack both zone
and man-to-man goal line coverages

Diagram 16-13 provides an example of a goal line offense play call chart. It should be noted that the first two posted run plays are listed similarly on the left and right side of the play call chart. There are times when an offensive coordinator may only want to run specific plays to the right or left side of the field. In the same vein, the 36 power pass play is listed only on the left side of the play call chart, with the play-action pass play only being called to the right. Why would the offensive coordinator limit the listing of such specific plays this way? It may be that the play is a crucial play situation, and the offensive coordinator only wants to throw that specific pass to the right, the quarterback's throwing side strong arm. On the other hand, perhaps, the offensive coordinator doesn't want to throw such a pass into the boundary, feeling that he may not have enough room in which that specific play to work.

❐ Runs:	
(13) Power Rt Tite 24 Ice	(13) Power Rt Tite 24 Ice
(13) Power Rt Tite 36 Power	(13) Power Rt Tite 36 Power
(11) Gun Weak Deuce Lt 20 Read	(11) Gun Weak Deuce Rt 21 Read
(12) Strong Wing Rt 8 Zone	(12) Strong Wing Lt 9 Zone
❐ Passes:	
(13) Power Rt Tite 36 Power Pass	
(13) Wing Rt Tite 2 Zone Naked Lt	(13) Wing Lt Tite 3 Zone Naked Rt
(11) Zoom Lt Trips Sprint-Out Cat	(11) Zoom Rt Trips Sprint-Out Cat
(0) Empty Lt Fly Sprint-Out China	(0) Empty Rt Fly Sprint-Out China
(10) Trey Rt Off 90 Chair	(10) Trey Lt Off 90 Chair
(11) Trips Lt 70 Chair P.C.	(11) Trips Rt 70 Chair P.C.

Diagram 16-13. An example of a goal line offense play call chart

Creating a Goal Line Two-Point Play Game Plan

The pressure is on. The offense has just scored to help put the offensive coordinator's team in position to tie, or win, the game at hand. But first, the offense must successfully convert a two-point play effort, with only seconds remaining on the game clock. Going for two points and the win can, in itself, can be a complex decision for whoever is the true decision-maker in such a scenario. As a result, when a team says it's going with the two-point play, the question is, then, does the team run the ball, pass it, or utilize some form of trick play? The answer should already be on the coordinator's play call chart—well-prepared and ready to go.

Prior to and during the practice week, the two-point play calls must already be well-established. The personnel and formation action must be ready to go. The plays must be well-taught and well-coached to the players by the offensive coaching staff. The decision of the actual two-point play to be used (e.g., run, pass, or trick play) should have been determined long ago. Furthermore, all factors considered, practicing such plays should blend in with the mechanics of the offense's goal line offense's efforts. In that regard, two-point plays should be taught and coached as the very last plays of goal line offense practice. As such, an argument can also be made to make a two-point play the last play practiced on the last offensive play of the practice week.

Should the offense utilize a run or a pass? If the coordinator's offense has overpowered the opposing defense all game long with the run game, and he feels confident that he has a goal line run play that can do the job, then, by all means, he should run the ball. The only question about a single, one-man run attempt is that in the confines of the situation's short-yardage needs, the defense may, very well, be able to overload the front at the line of scrimmage entry points of the ballcarrier. Still, a well-executed dive, power play, or sweep may be all that is needed to get the football over the goal line.

Run-option plays are also an excellent alternative for two-point play offense, especially if the offense has a good run-option package that is a normal part of its total offensive package. As such, a good run-option team should feel confident in its run-option attack, no matter where it is positioned on the field and/or what the game situation is. Run-option attacks have the advantage of forcing defenses to be assignment-oriented. Since goal line defenses can have varied alignments and assignments when they're assignment orientated, an assignment mistake by even one defender can quickly turn into a two-point conversion. This factor can be quite true, whether the run-option action is read-option, veer, I-option, wishbone, trap option, or any other form of run-option. As a result, creating two-on-one or three-on-two run-option designs can help put tremendous stress on assignment-oriented defenders.

Two-point play pass offense can, likewise, put tremendous pressure on two-point play defenses. Passing to a three-receiver goal line pass pattern gives the quarterback three potential targets that, in themselves, could be successful two-point plays. Just as in normal goal line situations, the emphasis should definitely be on the various modes of quickly designed pass throws. Quarterback sprint-out or move-out actions can also add to the threat of a successful, two-point score play by having the quarterback be the third, or fourth, two-point play threat with his ability to run the ball into the end zone, as shown in Diagram 16-14.

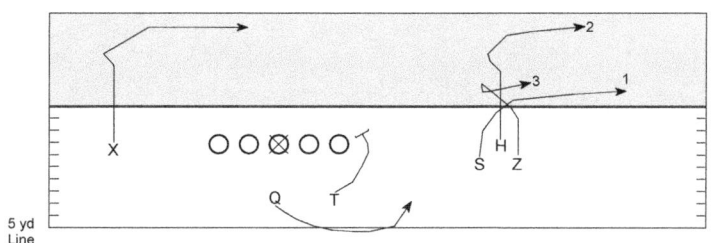

Diagram 16-14. Quarterback sprint-out pass action creating four potential two-point scoring threats

Diagram 16-15 provides an example of a short two-point, offense play call chart. It should be noted that there are, at least, two such two-point plays (a third is, certainly, possible) on a two-point offensive play call chart. Whether running the ball straight at a goal line defense, using run-option offense, or passing the football, the two-point play offensive package must be well thought-out, designed, taught, coached, and practiced. As a rule, the success or failure of that last, two-point play will, almost always, be the difference between a successful win or a crushing defeat. As such, the offensive coordinator and his staff must do everything they can to succeed in the pressure-filled, game-on-the-line, two-point play situation.

❒ Plays:

(11) Soar Weak Bunch Rt 70 Z Follow
(11) Zoom Weak Lt Trips Sprint Rt Cat
(11) Flip Strong Trey Rt 48 Throwback QB

Diagram 16-15. Two-point offensive play call chart

CHAPTER 17
PLANNING A COMING-OUT OFFENSE

The previous four chapters addressed the "big four" concepts of game planning: par (base) down offense, third-down offense, red zone offense, and goal line offense. At this point, it is appropriate to look at the supplemental, but no less important, remaining game-plan situations, including coming-out offense; four-minute slow/slow offense; last-play offense; and desperation offense.

Each of the aforementioned supplemental game-plan situations must be attended to with the same focus and concentration as any of the "big four" game plans. On one hand, they may not need the quantity of time attention that par (base) down offense or third-down offense need. On the other hand, if a coordinator/playcaller were asked how important a coming-out situation is, when his offense is backed up to his own two-yard line in the fourth quarter of a 21-21 playoff, championship football game, he might be wishing he had spent a lot more specific planning and practice time on the ever-critical coming-out situation. The bottom line is to be well-planned and well-practiced for each of the following supplemental game-plan situations.

The Critical, Coming-Out Offense Game Plan Situation

Coming-out offense is an extremely critical game plan situation. As the previous example alluded to, the word "critical" says it all. If the offense succeeds, the offense gets itself out of a deep, field-position yardage hole. A successful explosive run or pass play can be very devastating to the opponent's defense, as well as to the entire opposing team. Failure in executing coming-out offense means punting the ball and, quite possibly, turning the ball over to the opposition in great field position. Furthermore, if the coming-out offense is unable to get the football to, at least, the four-yard line, the offense might be forced to utilize the less-desired tight punt formation.

A tight punt formation can hinder the punt coverage to a much greater degree rather than the desired spread punt formation. A tight punt formation forces the punter to punt from a much closer distance to the line of scrimmage. This scenario creates a shorter distance for the defense's punt block efforts, given that the punter is backed-up to the out-of-bounds end line. In addition, devastating failure can occur, for example, a tackle of the ballcarrier in the end zone or a blocked punt that goes out the back of the end zone, as it crosses the end line. Both actions result in a two-point safety and a safety kick to the opposition from the offense's 20-yard line.

The immediate, realistic goal of a backed-up, coming-out offense is to get two first downs to put the offense in less dangerous field position, beyond the offense's own 20. Of course, a long, "explosive" run or pass gain would be an even better scenario. In addition, getting out beyond the 20-yard line gives the offensive coordinator a greater ability and a stauncher level of confidence to utilize all, or, at least, most of his offensive game plan.

A tight, well-thought out, well-practiced coming-out play call plan helps to eliminate the feeling of hopelessness and defeat. Instead, a sound, efficient coming-out game plan helps the offensive coordinator to call coming-out situational plays that have been well-practiced and are ready to go on the attack to otherwise succeed in such a difficult game-situation position.

The offensive coordinator must be sure to instill in his players feelings of grit and determination to handle this critical, game-type situation successfully. While the offensive players tend to be aware that their backs might very well be against the wall, they must be made to believe that such game situations can be handled effectively, because of solid game preparation and practice.

The offensive coordinator must not take the coming-out offense lightly. As a rule, the coming-out offense doesn't commonly happen. When it does, however, the magnitude of coming-out offense definitely comes to the forefront. Once the coming-out offense is installed early in the pre-season, it should then be coached and practice intently at least weekly. During a game week, the same premise applies.

As such, the offensive coordinator should have a relatively small, standard coming-out package that he feels will be a solid coming-out game-plan answer versus most any form of defensive attack. From there, he can make small or, possibly, large, coming-out run or pass play call additions or deletions to formulate the best coming-out play call game plan versus each specific opponent.

Creating a Coming-Out Offense Play Call Game Plan

On game-plan situations, such as goal line and short-yardage offense, there are many different theories on how to approach coming-out play call attacks. The first theory is the one that is definitely conservative in nature. It entails using tight ends and wing backs, which helps to prevent short, defensive rush edges from the outside, in an effort by the defense to squeeze the offensive backfield to the inside, whether the offensive plays are runs or passes. A relatively short path to the quarterback and running backs, due to a lack of extra tight ends or wing backs, can, surely, be devastating to any offense's run or pass efforts. Diagram 17-1 illustrates the use of extra tight ends and wing backs to eliminate short, outside rush edges by defensive end/outside linebacker/strong safety-type defenders.

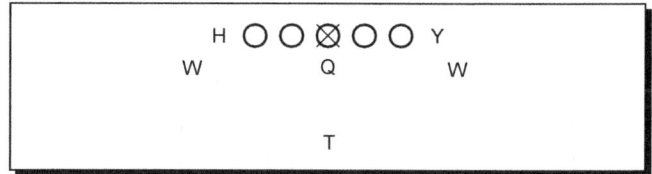

Diagram 17-1. The use of extra tight ends and wing backs to eliminate short defensive rush edges

Beefing up the offense with heavy, offensive personnel is another key, coming-out offensive concept. In reality, utilizing extra tight ends to eliminate short, defensive rush corners is also a way to employ extra heavy personnel for coming-out offense. An extra tackle on the line of scrimmage and an extra lineman in the backfield to bulk up run play blocking are other methods to beef up coming-out offensive formations. Diagram 17-2 illustrates the use of an extra offensive guard and tackle to beef up a tight, coming-out offensive formation.

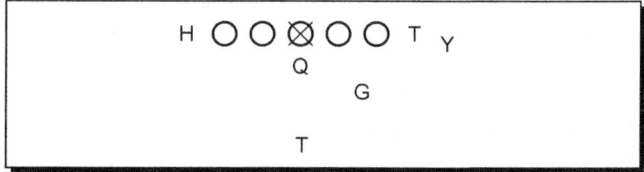

Diagram 17-2. The use of an extra guard and a tackle to beef up a coming-out offensive formation

As such, a number of offensive coordinators will simply use their best par (base) down offensive run and pass plays for their coming-out offense. The word "best" is very important with regard to whatever those designated best plays are. Coming-out offense is not the situation to experiment or get fancy. Power kick-out run plays, sweeps, isolation/blast plays, quick dives, and belly plays can be excellent coming-out run plays.

One adjustment that could be made is for the offensive coordinator to use his base, par down offense and bulk up the blocking in key blocking areas of the plays with extra offensive linemen, fullbacks, tight ends, and wing backs. One concern for coming-out run plays is pitches and tosses. A poor pitch or toss could quickly end up as a safety or a touchdown for the opposition.

No matter what the type of run utilized, the run plays should be those that have little chance of producing negative yardage. For that reason, an offensive coordinator should think twice about utilizing counter and reverse run plays. With defenses working hard to penetrate past the line of scrimmage to disrupt pulling offensive linemen, the coordinator must be sure that his run counter plays are stout when blocking down to the inside with angle blocking to seal penetration efforts, as well as being efficient when pulling to kick-out and lead the counter back runner.

When choosing an offense's best run or pass plays, the offensive coordinator should consider which side of the field to which to call a play. When I was coaching at the University of Idaho, we had the best power pulling guard I had ever coached. His name is Mike Iupati. Mike became the number one draft choice of the San Francisco 49ers and an All-Pro guard. Whenever I called an off-tackle power play in a critical situation, the power play was always to the right, and Big Mike was always the pulling guard leading the way.

A key coming-out run play is the quarterback sneak, especially if the football is on the one-yard line or less. There must be ample practice of the quarterback sneak with the wedge blocking of the offensive line. Obviously, the quarterback sneak can have many strategic uses during the course of a game.

The quarterback might even decide to execute a two-man, surprise "goose" sneak. On a "goose" sneak, the quarterback presses his spread hands under the center's rump to signal the "goose" snap. The pressure of the quarterback's hands actually comes from the bottom hand of the quarterback, making sure that the heels of the top and bottom hand do not separate until the snapped football is delivered.

If the offensive coordinator employs a run option-oriented offense, there should be little reason for him to change to other types of run-actions. Once again, double- and triple-option actions can put opposing defenses in a bind with regard to being assignment-oriented, rather than gap control-oriented. The major concern for a run option-oriented offense in a coming-out offense situation is a poor pitch or a poor exchange action. Such action can cause a safety, if the ballcarrier is tackled in the end zone. Furthermore, if the football is fumbled in the end zone, a recovery by the defense will result in a touchdown for the opposition.

Conversely, a positive for run-option action in the coming-out zone is that it can invite short-corner alignments by the defense for quicker developing pitch-action. In addition, the concern for outside keep/pitch action is what can help a triple option, dive-type play rip upfield quickly and explosively, in a north/south direction. Such triple option effectiveness can gain enough coming-out offense to force the defense to back off and play with more conventional base down defense.

On the other hand, pass-oriented offensive coordinators should not shy away from their basic pass- and run-play designs, as well. This factor is especially true for the pass game, if the defense tries to load up to attack a coming-out offense's run game. Once again, the coordinator should utilize his best, most secure pass and run plays.

A number of offensive coordinators will shy away from using much of their passes, in fear of sacks in the end zone producing a safety. This concern is certainly valid. Quick-game passing can be an effective way to get out of the coming-out zone, since a short, quick game pass completion, in itself, can help to get a coming-out offense out of danger.

Once again, utilizing a team's best, most highly efficient passes that allow the quarterback to get the passed football off quickly is a definite key. Furthermore, sprint-out or move out-type passes can help the quarterback to run away from approximately half of the backside pass rush via the quarterback's move-out action. What the offensive coordinator should avoid is delayed, straight back, dropback action, for which the offensive blockers have to hold their blocks for an extended period of time. As such, it is important for the offensive coordinator to be aware that a sack will, almost always, produce a safety. In that regard, quick, play-action passes can also be very effective in a coming-out situation, while longer/deeper play-action passes may not.

Bootleg, naked, and waggle-type actions can also be effective in coming-out situations. Much like the counter action that these play-action pass plays are by design, however, the offensive linemen must be able to do a great job of angle blocking to seal off any defensive penetration efforts.

All-in-all, the offensive coordinator can very well find that coming-out offense can be somewhat of a crap shoot. Very simply, he might be in the sixth week of the season and not have seen any examples of coming-out offenses versus opposing defenses. What does he do then? The best answer is to study the opposition's par (base) defense and their third-and-short defenses. If anything, the offensive coordinator should favor the use of two tight end formations to prevent short-corner, defensive-pressure actions. In addition, he should look for any defensive personnel weaknesses that might serve him well to attack. A weak defensive end? He should run his power kick-out play, or his sweep. Perhaps, that defensive end is the best defender to attack with the offense's run-option plays. The defense is weak covering passes? How about a slant or a hitch-and-go pass?

Special, trick plays can also be extremely effective for a coming-out offense, although they can be a bit of a gamble, as well. For example, a double pass or a throwback pass to a quarterback on a wheel route can produce a large chunk of yardage to get a fired-up, coming-out offense out of a big hole. All factors considered, in this situation, it might be best for the offensive coordinator to utilize special, trick plays that unfold to the outside, away from the defensive interior. Again, miscues in the offensive backfield area (the end zone) can easily result in a touchdown or a safety for the opponent. Diagram 17-3 provides an example of a coming-out play call chart.

❐ Runs:

(12) Wing Rt Yac Sneak Rt	(12) Wing Lt Yac Sneak Lt
(12) Wing Lt Twins 37 Power/92 Check	(12) Wing Rt Twins 36 Power/92 Check
(12) Strong Wing Rt Tite 48 Sweep	(12) Strong Wing Lt Tite 49 Sweep
(11) Zoom Pistol Trey Rt 21 Read	(11) Zoom Pistol Trey Lt 20 Read
(12) Strong Wing Rt Tite 24 Ice	(12) Strong Wing Lt Tite 25 Ice

❐ Passes:

(11) Pistol Deuce Lt 92 (Sluggo)	(11) Pistol Deuce Rt 92 (Sluggo)
(22) Strong Rt Tite 36 Power Pass	(22) Strong Lt Tite 37 Power Pass
(11) Pistol Trips Lt Max 90 Bench	(11) Pistol Trips Rt Max 90 Bench

---

Diagram 17-3. An example of a coming-out play call chart

Inspiring Coming-Out Offense Effectiveness

Whatever the offensive coordinator decides to do with regard to his coming-out offensive play call package, he must find a way to ensure that his offense is on the attack. Far too often, coaches and players have a tendency to mentally "go into the tank," when put in such a situation, when what is needed is a "let's-take-it-to-them" attitude.

Whether it's that coming-out offense, third-and-20, or "hurry/hurry" offense, these key, critical game challenges must be so well emphasized and focused upon in a team's teaching and coaching that the offense will have great confidence in gaining success. Practicing (for example) for a 10-minute period every Wednesday in periods 5 and 6 (five-minute periods) can help ensure that a level of stability exists when the all-important, critical, coming-out offense game situation occurs. When it does, the players must have a confident, "we've been here before; let's get the job done again!" attitude.

CHAPTER 18
PLANNING A FOUR-MINUTE, SLOW/SLOW OFFENSE

The football has just been punted to the offensive coordinator's team. The game clock reads 4:03. The offensive coordinator checks the scoreboard and sees that his opponent has two timeouts left. The football is on the offense's 41-yard line. The coordinator's team has a two-point lead. As such, it's time for his team's four-minute, slow/slow offense.

I recently watched an exciting NCAA football game in which one team had a small lead after blowing a large lead. They were still in charge, however, with that small lead and needed only to effectively utilize their four-minute, slow/slow offense to ensure a victory. Unfortunately, it quickly became relatively easy to see that the offense either didn't have a four-minute, slow/slow offense ready to go, or they simply were not very good at executing it. The quarterback was ignoring the time on the play clock and squandering the opportunity to use up valuable play-clock time with his snapping mechanics. On sweep action, the ballcarrier could easily have purposely fallen to the ground inside of the sideline to keep the clock ticking. On quarterback scrambling action, the quarterback threw the football out of bounds, when he could have easily run for a modest five- or six-yard gain and kept the clock ticking off valuable seconds.

No matter what the time remaining on the game clock, the critical situation four-minute, slow/slow offense must use up the remaining time on the game clock to help win the game or, to at least, turn the ball over to the opponent with as little time on the game clock as possible. These are the core goals of four-minute, slow/slow offense. It is now up to the offense to burn up that game clock time by maintaining possession of the football for as long as it can and/or until the referee declares the game over.

The best way to accomplish the basic objectives of four-minute, slow/slow offense is to successfully run the football, while keeping the football inbounds. It's time for the offense to "buckle-up their chin straps" and forcefully and powerfully drive the football forward, keeping it inbounds, until the game clock runs out of seconds. The offense must understand fully that their success will lead to victory.

The four-minute, slow/slow offense should anticipate the defensive pressure associated with red zone defense. The defense is in a precarious situation. It has to get the ball back. It has to apply some form of pressure to quickly produce a stop and take over possession of the football. Blitz? Bring pressure off the corners?

A major problem that an offensive coordinator might face in this situation is that he may not have any game opponent video of defending a four-minute, slow/slow offense. As such, analyzing his opponent's red zone defense may help give him his best tips concerning how to best execute his four-minute, slow/slow offense. If he's still unsure, he should consider starting out by using a two-tight end formation to ensure that there are no short corners for defensive ends/outside linebackers/strong safeties to exploit. Such a two-tight formation to ensure that there are no short corners for the defense to exploit is illustrated in Diagram 18-1.

Diagram 18-1. Two-tight end formation to help eliminate short corner defensive rushes

Four-Minute, Slow/Slow Offense Mechanics

There are several very important rules and concepts that must be adhered to by the offensive coordinator when his team is in a four-minute, slow/slow offensive situation. For example, when utilizing his snap count at the line of scrimmage, the quarterback must use up as much of the play clock time as possible. At the college and professional levels, a play clock is utilized to tell the quarterback how much time he has before he executes his snap. On the high school level, where such play clocks are rarely on the field, the quarterback needs for the referee standing over the football to start his last five seconds count verbally and/or with a waving hand. Such referee action informs the quarterback of the last five seconds before the play clock runs out.

Furthermore, when running with the football, the ballcarrier must do all he can to stay inbounds in order to not stop the clock. In that regard, the ballcarrier should go as far as diving or falling to the ground to keep the clock ticking. The basic concept is quite clear…don't run out of bounds. The lone exception can be running out of bounds to gain first-down yardage, which will give the offense a fresh, new, set of downs. A new first down greatly increases the offense's chances of burning up the time still remaining on the game clock.

The next key concept in this situation is for any free offender to purposely fall on top of the downed ballcarrier to help produce a stack of offensive players on top of the ballcarrier. The underlying premise in this situation is for the stacked offensive players to get up off the pile slowly, one-by-one, off of the ballcarrier, similar to an onion being peeled, one layer at a time. Such a stacking and unstacking action can, definitely, but within reason, help to eat up precious seconds on the game clock.

With regard to "within reason," offensive players in the area of the down ballcarrier falling on top of him is "within reason." What is not "within reason?" It is not "within reason" when the referee throws a flag for such stalling action. Once the referee starts to threaten that he will throw a flag, it's definitely time for any remaining offensive players to get up off the pile.

Creating a Four-Minute, Slow/Slow Offense Play Call Game Plan

Once again, formationing can be an essential aspect of four-minute, slow/slow offense. For example, having a tight end on each end of the formation can be very helpful for inside-type run plays to prevent the defense having short corner edge rushing. Being one offender wider in creating such a short-edge corner, with a tight end blocker, is a major way to stretch the defense and prevent rush pressure from the outside.

If the four-minute, slow/slow offense is utilizing sweep or sprint-out type action in its efforts to eat up the clock, extra tight ends/fullbacks/wingbacks can be effectively used to protect the outside running ballcarrier. The ballcarrier must be ready to fall to the ground inbounds to help keep the game clock moving, unless the ballcarrier can easily gain first yardage and earn a fresh, new set of downs. Diagram 18-2 illustrates the use of extra tight end and wingback to help block the corner for a quarterback sweep.

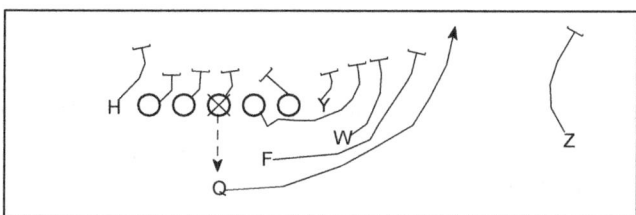

Diagram 18-2. Using an extra tight end and wing back for a quarterback sweep

Run-option action can help to stretch the ballcarrier's run actions out wide in an effort to further use up the game clock. One of the key concerns for run-option action is the pressuring action of defense in their desperate efforts to force a turnover. Pressure on the pitch-option action can easily lead to the possibility of the football being fumbled. Penetration action by the defense can also create the possibility of a fumble in the more open area behind the line of scrimmage that can produce both a fumble recovery and a scoop-and-score situation for the opposition. If an offense is firmly based in run-option football, however, it should have the confidence in its run, keep, and pitch option abilities to attack in any key game situation, as opposed to just relying on its four-minute, slow/slow offense. On the other hand, if an offense has a once-in-a-while read-option-type play in its arsenal, the offensive coordinator should think twice about the possibility of using such a play. If the offense is based in run-option, it should carefully employ its best run-option actions.

With the game on-the-line, the offensive coordinator should, again, use his best runs from his running-game arsenal. Quick-hitting run plays that can have the ability to burst through the line of scrimmage should be of high priority on the offensive coordinator's four-minute, slow/slow play call list. In addition, he should avoid run-game plays that are susceptible to producing lost yardage behind the line of scrimmage. Counter action is a run action that can be dangerous due to penetration action from the defensive front players. On the other hand, counter action in four-minute, slow/slow offensive situations can be an excellent way to take advantage of an overpursuing defense.

Diagram 18-3 illustrates a waggle quarterback sweep, with faking action to the left. A backside pulling guard and blocking action by the two playside wide receivers helps to secure a slow-developing run play that has the potential to run off a significant amount of game clock time. Just as in any outside run action, the quarterback must be sure to stay inbounds, in order to keep the clock running.

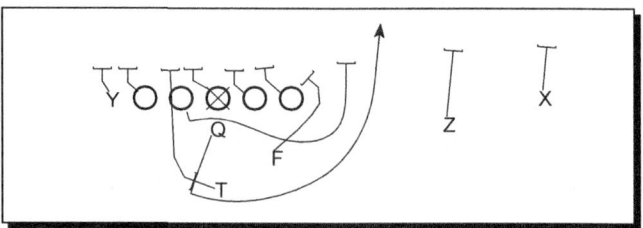

Diagram 18-3. Waggle quarterback sweep action

The coordinator could also call for, simply, a waggle counter-action pass play. Such waggle action has the backside pulling guard for blocking security and either the potential of an open throw to the waggle-pattern receivers or the opportunity for a quarterback keep-run action. Such waggle-run, quarterback-keep action, with potential waggle pass-action, is shown in Diagram 18-4. Again, a catching receiver must be sure not to run out of bounds, unless such action will cleanly produce first-down yardage.

Furthermore, the quarterback must keep in mind that when in doubt, he should run the football, being careful to stay inbounds, unless his run-action can easily produce a first down.

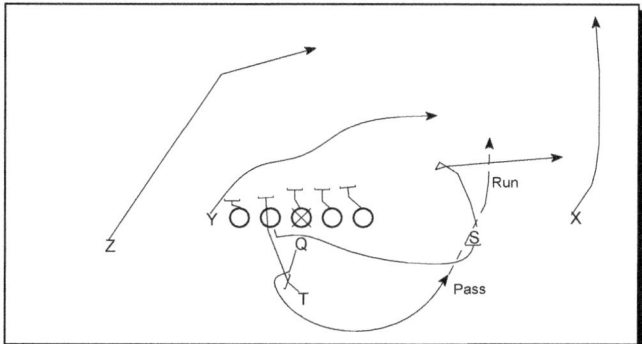

Diagram 18-4. Waggle run/pass-action

The passing game is a different story for four-minute, slow/slow offense. The key issue in this situation, of course, is that an incomplete pass stops the clock. Passing on third- or fourth-down situations can be the exception. Teams that are good passing teams might feel that passing the football can be a strong possibility on par (base) down situations. On the other hand, the risk of an incompletion and a stopped game clock can quickly lead the offensive coordinator to regret making such a play call.

If the offensive coordinator feels he needs to make a passing play call, he should pick one that is likely to be the most effective, as well as the easiest to execute. In reality, many coaches like to move the quarterback in this passing situation to help the quarterback to hopefully avoid the backside half of a pass rush. Sprint, move-out, and misdirection bootleg/waggle actions can all help to get the quarterback out on the perimeter, with an excellent chance to complete a pass or to run for significant yardage.

Quick, three-step, timed short passes can also be sound play calls in this situation. In addition, RPOs (run/pass options) can be extremely successful in four-minute, slow/slow offense, if the quarterback is effective in making such run/pass reads. Diagram 18-5 presents an example of a four-minute, slow/slow offense play call chart.

❐   Runs:

(22) Strong Rt Tite Sweep Rt	(22) Strong Lt Tite Sweep Lt
(12) Weak Rt Tite 36 Power	(12) Weak Lt Tite 37 Power
(11) Pistol Deuce Lt 20 Read	(11) Pistol Deuce Rt 21 Read
(12) Weak Lt Twins 3 Waggle Rt Keep	(12) Weak Rt Twins 2 Waggle Lt Keep
(12) Doubles Rt Zone Check	(12) Doubles Lt Zone Check
(12) Shift Unbalanced Rt 47 Load	(12) Shift Unbalanced Lt 46 Load
(11) Zoom Lt Trips Fly Sweep Rt	(11) Zoom Rt Trips Fly Sweep Lt

❐   Passes:

(11) Rt Trey 90 Hitch or Bench	(11) Lt Trey 90 Hitch or Bench
(12) Doubles Rt 70 X-Ray	(12) Doubles Lt 70 X-Ray
(11) Gun Trey Rt Sprint Rt Zorro	(11) Gun Trey Lt Sprint Lt Zorro
(11) Lt Weak Deuce Zoom Sprint Rt Dog	(11) Rt Weak Deuce Zoom Sprint Lt Dog

Diagram 18-5. An example of a four-minute, slow/slow offensive play call chart

CHAPTER 19
PLANNING A TWO-MINUTE, HURRY/HURRY OFFENSE

The two-minute, hurry/hurry offense situation is one of the most game critical offensive situations in all of football. The offensive coordinator's team needs 40 yards to put his field goal kicker in a reasonable yardage position to kick a field goal to win, or tie, the football game. There is 1:37 on the game clock, and his team has two time-outs remaining. Or, his team is behind by six points. His team has only one time-out, with only 1:59 on the game clock. In close scoring football games, the two-minute, hurry/hurry offense becomes the final push for a needed score, be it for the first half of the game or for the points needed to tie or win a game.

In finishing the game, this is it. The offensive coordinator's team executes its two-minute, hurry/hurry offense and either wins, or ties the game to go into overtime (including, possibly, a needed extra-point kick to make the difference). As much pressure as has been placed on both teams during the course of the game and on the coaches and fans, the newest excitement has built like a crescendo. The game is on the line "…right now!" Can the coordinator and quarterback help lead the team to a victory or will the offense shut down, leading to a defeat. Previously in this book, a case was built for par (base) down offense, third-down offense, red zone offense, and goal line offense as the "big four" of game planning segments, practice, and play calling. If a fifth segment were added to make it the "big five," it would definitely be two-minute, hurry/hurry offense.

Two-Minute, Hurry/Hurry Thinking

The two-minute, hurry/hurry offense must be well-designed, well-planned, well-practiced, and well-executed. The two-minute, hurry/hurry design and plan should start out with a small, but sound, group of easy-to-execute run and pass plays that can be smoothly utilized in an on-the-line situation against almost any defensive structure. These run and pass plays should all come from the "big four" play calling segments and should be some of the best and, hopefully, most efficient run and pass plays to execute from the offense's big four play call lists. The short, condensed, on-the-line, two-minute, hurry/hurry play call plan should be clearly understood. It should help to reinforce an inner feeling of confidence by the offensive players involved in their team's game-on-the-line, two-minute, hurry/hurry actions.

Two-minute, hurry/hurry offense planning should focus on gaining chunks of yardage. For the most part, that's where the passing game comes in. On the other hand, unless the offense is in a near-desperation situation, due to an extremely brief period of two-minute, hurry/hurry time and still having a long way to go to get in the end zone, the offense should consider utilizing controlled passing that can exploit zone, man-to-man, and prevent coverages.

The offensive coordinator and quarterback should throw to routes, such as a slant or a crossing route, that allow a receiver to run for valuable yardage after the actual catch of the football. Furthermore, the offensive coordinator should utilize pass plays that, in themselves, have built-in blitz-beaters in the two-minute, hurry/hurry pass patterns being utilized. The offense could also have built-in sight adjustment systems to take on defensive blitzes, if the opponents blitz in this pressing game situation.

An excellent consideration, especially if the two-minute, hurry/hurry offense has a long way to go, is to focus on getting two first downs in a reasonably quick amount of time. In this situation, a number of defenses start to think about employing prevent-type coverages. Prevent coverages can be exploited with medium-distance completions in the 10-yard range, whether the throws, themselves, produce a 10-yard completion or put the receivers in a position to run for 10 or so yards, after the receiver makes his reception. Such a concept helps the offense to quickly gain 20 plus yards in the two-minute, hurry/hurry offense. Most importantly, two first down helps to provide vital momentum on which the two-minute, hurry/hurry offense can build.

Two-Minute, Hurry/Hurry Communication

Much of on-the-line, two-minute, hurry/hurry success depends on communication. Clear, distinct, and precise communication must be used from the offensive coordinator to a signaling field coach, or coaches, to the quarterback, as well as to the on-the-field players. The quarterback must receive the desired plays clearly from the communicating field coach, or coaches, either using hand signals or with coded large placards/signs held over a student manager's head. In reality, the signaling action to the quarterback could be accomplished by more than one field coach or with a placard/sign holder acting as dummy signalers. Some teams use two field signalers—one to signal in the personnel plan and formation and another to signal the actual play to the quarterback.

From that point, the quarterback must turn to one side of the field to yell out the sideline play call to the widest receiver. He then scans the field to the opposite side of the field, checking to be sure that the formation is correct. Finally, he then yells out his play call to the widest receiver, aligned to the opposite side of the field. If the widest receiver to each side of the formation can clearly hear the quarterback's play call, then all players inside of the widest receivers should be able to clearly hear the play call as well. The other communications option is for all of the offensive players on the field to get the play call from the sideline signal caller(s).

Creating an On-the-Line, Two-Minute, Hurry/Hurry Offense Play Call Plan

Creating a two-minute, hurry/hurry offense play call plan starts with the use of basic, on-the-line formation usage. Since an offense is dealing with a limited amount of seconds, utilizing one personnel/formation plan is an extremely effective approach. By using (for example) a 10 personnel, four-wide receiver, two-by-two formation, the quarterback only has to call out "…on-the-line, right, right…" or "…on-the-line, left, left…" to get the 10 personnel receivers and single running back in a correct alignment with, or without, the receivers switching sides.

In reality, the offensive coordinator might feel more comfortable using a tight end, 11 personnel plan. One way of the other, 10 or 11 personnel plans can easily adjust to balanced, two-by-two formations. Three-by-one formations can also be effective in on-the-line, two-minute, hurry/hurry situations, as well. On the other hand, there can be greater difficulties for three-by-one formations, with regard to difficulties flipping formation alignments, when going from one hash to the other.

The plays (as a rule, more pass plays than run plays for the on-the-line, two-minute, hurry/hurry game plan) should show a balance of dropback and move-out (sprint-out/roll-out/dash/bootleg) pass-actions. If the only passing a two-minute, hurry/hurry offense employs is straight dropback action, the defense will be in a better position to tee-off and aggressively pass rush the consistent, behind-the-center launch point. As such, having a mixture of dropback and move-out launch points puts extra pressure on a pass rushing defense.

The quick pass game is an excellent, on-the-line, two-minute, hurry/hurry play call plan with which to start out. The only problem with using the quick pass game is that the gains can be short, which results in using up valuable time on the clock for such short yardage gains. Slants, however, can be extremely effective, since the football is often caught while the receiver is on the run. Throwing to hitches and quick out-routes should also be considered, when putting together the on-the-line, two-minute, hurry/hurry game plan, to see if they can be yardage-effective in this pressing game situation.

For the most part, five-step dropback action enables medium- and deep-level passes to be thrown, without necessitating prolonged pass protection. Again, patterns with built-in, blitz-beater routes can be very important, as are sight-adjust designs to help defeat blitzes. Move passes help to eliminate a good portion of a backside pass rush, as well as put the quarterback in a position to effectively run the football, if all pass routes are covered. Play-action passes can, at times, also be helpful. On the other hand, linebackers may be less willing to suck up on run fakes due to nickel- and dime-type pass coverages, thereby negating the effectiveness of play-action passes.

A key, on-the-line, two-minute, hurry/hurry offense consideration is to have and utilize specific pass patterns that can attack zone coverage, man-to-man coverage, or a combination of both. On zone coverages, the on-the-line, two-minute, hurry/hurry offense looks to attack zone voids and flood-specific portions of such zone coverages. When they're facing man-to-man coverage, the offense should look to isolate specific man-to-man coverage defenders. The offense could also effectively utilize crossing route patterns versus man-to-man coverages. The key point to remember is that all of these defensive on-the-line, two-minute, hurry/hurry situations must be analyzed carefully from opponent video study, just as are all other game-planning situational needs.

Screen passes, a draw and, possibly, a run play or two (e.g., dive, draw, draw trap) that fit into an on-the-line, two-minute, hurry/hurry design being put together by the offensive coordinator and his staff help to round out the basic, overall plan. A key consideration in this situation is to, initially, have a basic, on-the-line, two-minute, hurry/hurry plan that is a tight, condensed plan that can be well-practiced and executed fluidly. It must be a plan that can successfully attack defensive efforts to prevent success for the offense. As such, a core, on-the-line plan can be added to, or have some plays deleted in an effort to best fit into the two-minute, hurry/hurry plays needed versus specific opponents. Diagram 19-1 illustrates an example of an on-the-line, two-minute, hurry/hurry play call chart.

Runs:	
(10) Deuce Lt 40 Trap	(10) Deuce Rt 41 Trap
(10) Deuce Lt 50 Draw	(10) Deuce Rt 51 Draw
(10) Deuce Lt 20 Read	(10) Deuce Rt 21 Read
Passes:	
(10) Deuce Lt 90 Hitch (Hugo)	(10) Deuce Rt 90 Hitch (Hugo)
(10) Deuce Lt 92 Slant (Sluggo)	(10) Deuce Rt 92 Slant(Sluggo)
(10) Deuce Lt 93 (and Up)	(10) Deuce Rt 93 (and Up)
(10) Deuce Lt 70 Dbl Acute/Option	(10) Deuce Rt 70 Dbl Acute/Option
(10) Deuce Lt 75 Cross	(10) Deuce Rt 75 Cross
(10) Weak Deuce Lt Sprint Rt Spider	(10) Weak Deuce Rt Sprint Lt Spider
(10) Deuce Lt 76 Dbl Post	(10) Deuce Rt 76 Dbl Post
(10) Deuce Lt 77 Smash	(10) Deuce Rt 77 Smash
(10) Deuce Lt 70 Verts	(10) Deuce Rt 70 Verts
(10) Weak Deuce Lt Sprint Rt Sail	(10) Weak Deuce Rt Sprint Lt Sail

Diagram 19-1. An example of a two-minute, hurry/hurry play call chart

One other concern, when planning a two-minute, hurry/hurry offense, is the clock stopping due to an incompletion or due to a ballcarrier running out-of-bounds, with the clock not restarting until the snap of the football on the next play. Offensive coordinators who run fast-paced offenses might, actually, ignore the fact that the clock has been stopped and continue into their fast-paced regimen.

Some coaches are of the opinion that the situation is an opportunity to take the advantage of the clock being stopped. They might feel that they will now have the time to recheck their total play call chart to see if there are some other play calls that might be particularly effective at that point of the two-minute, hurry/hurry drive. As such, a number of those coaches might have a "huddle-up" play call, listing on their play call charts to have additional plays calls ready for the "stop-the-clock," two-minute, hurry/hurry offense situations that they encounter. An example of a "huddle-up," two-minute, hurry/hurry offense play call chart is shown in Diagram 19-2.

Runs:	
(10) Pistol Deuce Lt 18 Speed Option	(10) Pistol Deuce Rt 19 Speed Option
Passes:	
(10) Trips Lt 74 Z Clear Max	(10) Trips Rt 74 Z Clear Max
(10) Pistol Deuce Lt 71 Y Option	(10) Pistol Deuce Rt 71 Y Option
(10) Pistol Deuce Lt DBL Squares	(10) Pistol Deuce Rt DBL Squares

Diagram 19-2. An example of a huddle-up, two-minute, hurry/hurry offense play call chart

CHAPTER 20
THE ALL-IMPORTANT SCRAMBLE PASS CONCEPT

The all-important scramble pass pattern concept is one of the shortest chapters in this book. On the other hand, it is certainly a very important offensive concept, especially if the offensive coordinator is a pass game-oriented coach and firmly believes in throwing the football. Unfortunately, in reality, a number of coaches totally ignore the importance of the scramble pass concept, including the need to practice it, whether they are pass-oriented coaches or not.

All factors considered, it can be helpful for every offensive coordinator to take some time to analyze whether or not he should be paying attention to the scramble pass concept. An appropriate first step for him, in this regard, would be to quickly view three, four, or five of his game videos from his passing-game breakdowns. He should check how many of his team's actual passing attempts end up being scramble passes. Two or three per game? Five or six?

Once he realizes how often the percentage is of his quarterback finding himself scrambling during the course of a game, he should then ask himself, does his quarterback know what to do once he's forced to scramble? Furthermore, just as importantly, he should ask himself whether his receivers know what to do once his quarterback starts to scramble? If the answers are "no, they don't," then a drastic need exists for him to teach, coach, and implement the scramble pass concept with his offense.

All factors considered, a scramble pass action should not be difficult to execute. Diagram 20-1 illustrates an example of scramble pass-action that I have used for many,

many years that has served me well as an offensive coordinator. While the scramble pass pattern concept could show a variety of scramble pattern designs, most coordinators stick to one, basic scramble pass pattern action to help facilitate consistency. The important factor, in this regard, is that the quarterback has a constant scramble pass pattern in front of him and that he knows how he will read/scan that pattern.

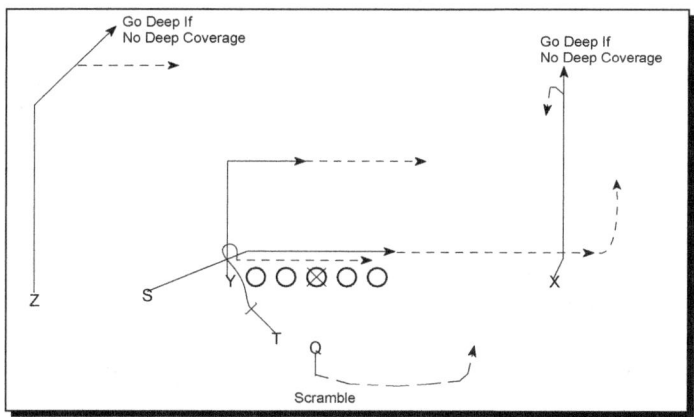

Diagram 20-1. An example of a scramble pass pattern concept

In Diagram 20-1, the quarterback is shown scrambling to his right. Anyone in the flat or the out-route area to the side of the scramble should turn upfield and run a deep streak route, looking over his inside shoulder. If a receiver is already deep to the outside and is not covered by a defender, he should continue going deep. If the deep receiver to the side of the scramble is covered deep, he should turn back toward the line of scrimmage, in an effort to come back to the scrambling quarterback.

Other receivers should flatten out their backside routes to trail the quarterback's scramble action, looking for zone voids, if the defensive coverage is zone. Zone voids refer to open zone windows into which the quarterback can safely throw. If the defensive coverage is man-to-man, the backside receivers should, initially, use man-to-man separation techniques to break away from the man-to-man coverage defenders. They should then work across the field at top speed to maintain that man-to-man coverage separation.

If a defender is tightly positioned to a covering, trailing route runner, the receiver should attempt to shake off the tight man-to-man coverage by "stair-stepping" upfield quickly for two or three steps and then breaking once again on a flattened-out route toward the sideline to which the quarterback is scrambling. The "stair-stepping" action should also be utilized if the receiver suddenly realizes he is closely following one of his own receivers. By "stair-stepping," the trailing receiver will be able to create a needed degree of separation from his own receiver who is in front of him, hopefully creating a new window into which the scrambling quarterback can throw. Diagram 20-2 illustrates "stair-stepping" action for a scramble pattern principle concept, when one receiver realizes he is too closely following a scrambling receiver from behind.

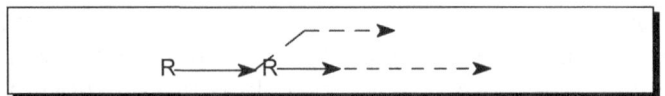

Diagram 20-2. Stair-stepping action for a scramble
pattern principle concept

Deep receivers on the backside of the scramble pattern should also work to the side of the quarterback's scramble action heavily by attempting to run deep, flattened-out, post route-type action, in an attempt to get into the scrambling quarterback's line of vision. The scrambling quarterback, being pursued from the backside by the defense, will usually not be able to find backside receivers, if such receivers don't break across the field hard to get into the quarterback's vision.

What happens if the quarterback suddenly breaks back toward the opposite sideline to continue executing his scramble action? The receivers should break back to the opposite side of the field, utilizing the same scramble route/pattern rules as detailed in Diagram 20-1. One way or another, the receivers should work hard to get into zone or man-to-man coverage voids to the side of the field to which the quarterback is scrambling.

The rules for scramble pattern route action are, in actuality, quite simplistic. When a receiver finds that he is a bit lost amidst the pattern concept, his colleague receivers and the defenders from the opposing team just run across the formation to the side the quarterback has scrambled to and find zone or man-to-man coverage voids to work into, within the quarterback's vision. Diagram 20-3 illustrates an example of a scramble action pattern/design.

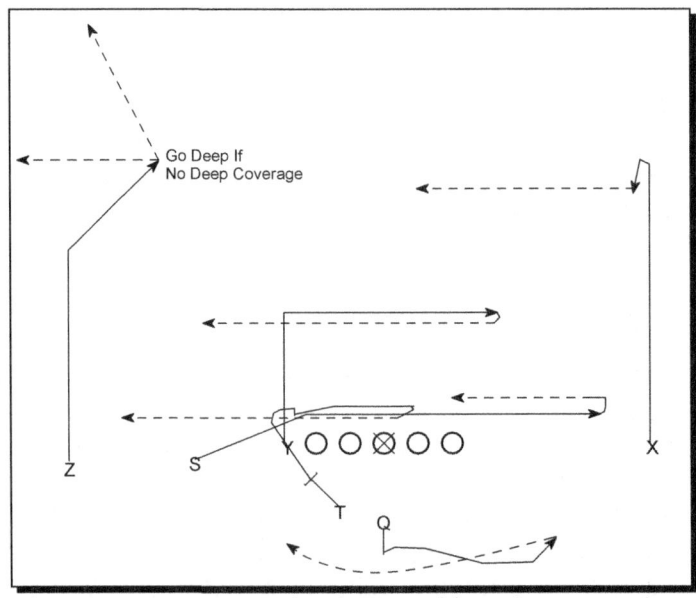

Diagram 20-3. An example of a scramble action pattern/
design, if the quarterback breaks back to the opposite side

It is essential that the offensive coordinator is realistic in the execution of the scramble concept. The receivers should have definite rules to follow for the scramble concept. On the other hand, the timing and field placement of the receivers in a scramble situation may not be exact amidst the mayhem of a quarterback running for his life and receivers who may not recognize in a timely fashion the fact that they are in a scramble situation. The overriding rule for any potential scramble receiver is to work to the side of the scrambling quarterback and create windows into which the quarterback can throw the football. Whatever the receivers are doing, they must not let underneath coverage defenders block the potential throwing pathways for the quarterback's attempts to throw a completed pass.

Practicing the Scramble Pass-Action

Practicing the scramble pass-action is relatively easy. The offensive coordinator can take a short five-minute period once a week, during the in-season, to enact the scramble pass rules off of a pass pattern that is already in motion. All factors considered, three or four repetitions by the first and second team offense, executing the scramble pass design is, often, an adequate amount of repetitions to be executed in such a short, five-minute time period.

Another way to practice scramble pass design action is for the offensive coordinator to pat, nod, or wink to his quarterback during a 7-on-7 pass drill or an 11-on-11 team drill, when a pass play is the next play to be practiced. The quarterback then sets up for the pass play called. Instead of executing the huddle call or an on-the-line play call, however, the quarterback breaks off to the left or right to enact the scramble pass concept. This tactic helps to create a more realistic effort of enacting the all-important scramble pass concept, since the forced scramble pass-action normally develops from a broken-down pass pattern and subsequent route action.

CHAPTER 21
PLANNING A
KILL-THE-CLOCK OFFENSE

The last two planning concepts for the offensive coordinator also deal with critical game situations: kill-the-clock offense and Hail-Mary offense (last-play offense). Both address the proper usage of the scant few seconds of a game, in the effort to either run out the game clock or to score vital points to win or tie a game. Chapter 21 covers kill-the-clock offense, while Chapter 22 discusses Hail-Mary offense.

Kill-The-Clock Offense Reasoning and Execution

The offense has just successfully executed its four-minute, slow/slow offense, using up the game clock to insure a victory. Or, has it? How much time is still on the game clock? Can the offense truly take a knee three times, or possibly a fourth time, to finish off those last few game-clock seconds to ensure the game win?" Offensive coordinators will confront situations in which such questions need answers quickly and correctly.

Above all, the offensive coordinator must be sure that he, himself, clearly understands the workings of his team's kill-the-clock offense. In that regard, he must understand that kill-the-clock offense may very well, and hopefully be, the ending extension of the offense's four-minute, slow/slow offense. On the other hand, his offense might be taking over his team's change of possession due to one of several factors, such as the opponent's failure to convert a first down on their own fourth down effort, a recovered fumble, or an interception. At that point, one way or the other, the offensive coordinator should examine his kill-the-clock offensive calculation chart that should be an integral part of his offensive play call chart.

The Kill-the-Clock Offensive Calculation Chart

The kill-the-clock offensive calculation chart helps to tell the offensive coordinator whether he can directly go into the offense's kill-the-clock offense. On the other hand, he may need extra game-clock time burnt up by his offense, before he is able to utilize his kill-the-clock offense. If compiled properly, the offensive coordinator should be able to quickly find out that information simply by looking at his kill-the-clock calculation chart.

The underlying premise of the kill-the-clock calculation chart is based on the assumption that the offense can burn up five seconds on a run play. In reality, that five-second period can, and usually does, get extended a few extra seconds as the officials spot the football. The second delaying factor is the slowness of the offensive players who find themselves laying on top of a downed ballcarrier. This action, in itself, can burn up vital, extra seconds, as other offensive players purposely attempt to cover the ballcarrier. Once again, such action to get up off the ballcarrier is slowly executed to burn up extra, vital game-clock seconds. If the referee is quick to spot the football, and extra players are not able to fall to the ground to cover the ballcarrier, the offensive coordinator can count on at least 15 seconds of time being used up on the game clock, even if the defense has all three of its time-outs remaining.

The other game clock time-burning factor that is a major part of the kill-the-clock calculation equation is that the offensive coordinator can rely on burning up 40 seconds for every time out that the opposing team doesn't have. If the game clock is almost totally expended, the offensive coordinator is still able to run out an additional five seconds on a fourth down run play or by having the quarterback back up and attempt to stand upright for a few extra seconds (kill-stay-alive), before taking a knee or purposely falling to the ground. Diagram 21-1 details an example of a kill-the-clock offensive calculation chart.

---

(3) Time-outs—15 seconds
(2) Time-outs—55 seconds
(1) Time-out—1:35
(0) Time-outs—2:15

Diagram 21-1. An example of a kill-the-clock offensive calculation chart

The Basic Kill-the-Clock Offensive Formation

There is very little variation in the main, basic formation utilized in kill-the-clock offense. The primary formation is a two-tight end formation intended to elongate the formation, so that wide, defensive rushers can't get to the quarterback on his take-a-knee action. Two blocking-type offenders (fullbacks/wing backs) position themselves snuggly toward the line of scrimmage in the "A" gaps, in an effort to prevent "A" gap penetration to disturb the center/quarterback exchange and, possibly, cause a fumble.

A key offender in the base kill-the-clock offense formation is the super-deep tailback, positioned 11 yards from the center. Generally, he is a running back or wide receiver who is quick, athletic, and has excellent hands. His job is to be a deep center fielder, with the prime job of fielding any snapped football that squirts past the quarterback for any variety of reasons. He is responsible for fielding any loose football. He does not try to pick up the football and run. He, simply, fields the errant football by folding over it, making sure he doesn't pounce on top of the football with the possibility of the football squirting out from underneath his body. The basic kill-the-clock formation is shown in Diagram 21-2.

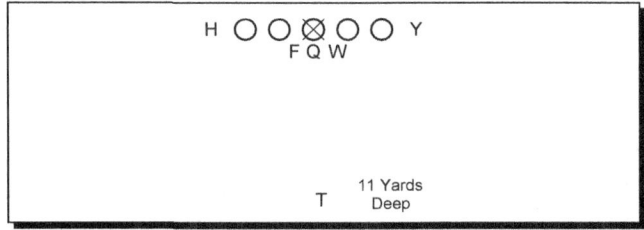

Diagram 21-2. Basic kill-the-clock formation

Kill-the-Clock Execution

There are two basic plays for the offensive coordinator to utilize in the kill-the-clock offense. The first kill-the-clock play is the take-a-knee play, in which the quarterback takes the snapped football from the center, and steps back away from the line of scrimmage for a foot or so. He steps behind the well-blocked area or pocket left by the tightly aligned offensive linemen and the second-level fullbacks, tight ends, or wingbacks. The quarterback then immediately bends down to touch his knee to the ground to end that particular play. The quarterback should, at that point, pop back up quickly and step backwards, away from the center area to hand the football to the referee. This step is undertaken, primarily, to avoid any possibility of flailing bodies falling on the quarterback's legs, risking an injury.

The take-a-knee play is called for by the offensive coordinator when there, simply, is not enough time on the clock for the opposition to get the football back. The particular reason for this scenario is the ability of the offense to execute one to three (maybe even four) kill-the-clock plays, as well as the amount of time on the game clock that can still be burned due to the lack of time-outs remaining for the opposition.

The second play, the kill-stay-alive play, is utilized when it is determined that the offense needs to burn a short, but significant, amount of the extra seconds that are remaining on the clock. On the kill-stay-alive play, the quarterback steps back one to two yards away from the line of scrimmage, after receiving the snap from the center. He then awaits the defense's forward rush, until the blocking of the line and second-level blockers begins to close in around him.

At that point, the quarterback purposely flops to the ground on his side to curl up around the football, securing it tightly to his stomach. Once the quarterback falls to the ground, the up-back offenders purposely fall on the quarterback one at a time in layers. The rationale for this tactic is that the up-back offenders will stay on top of one another, until the referees tell the offenders to "get up." These defenders then slowly get up off of the quarterback one at a time, as if they were layers of an onion, being peeled one layer at a time.

This slow-down action can help add valuable time being taken off the game clock. One key point to adhere to in this situation is that when the referee starts to say "get up or I'm going to throw a flag," it's truly time to start getting up off the pile.

Kill-Take-a-Safety

A third, and certainly different kill-the-clock play, is the kill-take-a-safety play. The kill-take-a-safety play involves a slightly different alignment than the one employed in the kill-the-clock formation. Instead of two A-gap offenders, who are normally aligned between the center and the guards, they are now aligned as wing backs. This repositioning is done to widen any possible defensive rushers from getting to the quarterback, as he executes a kill-take-a-safety play.

The super-deep tailback aligns at the normal 11 yards of the kill-take-a-knee and kill-stay-alive plays. Once the tailback sees the quarterback dropping back to execute his take-a-safety run course to the back end line of the end zone, the super-deep tailback steps up to the left, straddling behind the offensive tackle's inside foot (for a right-handed quarterback) to a position seven-yards deep from the center. The reset position for the tailback to the left is designed to put him into position to initially block any pressure coming from a right-handed quarterback's blindside. From that left alignment position, the tailback subsequently resets to a midline position, directly behind the center, to become a personal protector for the quarterback. He then scans and positions himself from left to right to block the first defender to break through the line of scrimmage in pursuit of the take-a-safety quarterback.

At this point, the take-a-safety quarterback sprints back to the end line, positioning himself a yard from it. From that position, he can sprint out of bounds to cause the safety, if he is being pursued heatedly from both sides. If he is only being heavily pursued by a defender from one side or another, the quarterback can then sprint along the end line toward the sideline to the opposite side of the defensive pressure, in an effort to eat up more game clock time. If the quarterback is not being pursued by the defense, he should stay at the straight back, dropback position, a yard from the end line, until a defender pressures him, in order to help continue burning up clock time. Once the quarterback decides to run out of bounds, he must sprint out of bounds to avoid taking a "big hit" from a defender. The kill-take-a-safety play is illustrated in Diagram 21-3.

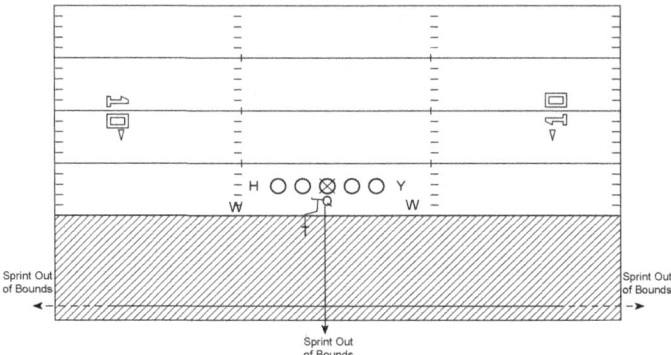

Diagram 21-3. Kill-take-a-safety formation and play

Kill-the-Clock Play Call Game Plan Chart

Diagram 21-4 provides an example of a kill-the-clock play call chart.

Kill-the-clock offense:
- Take-a-knee
- Kill-stay-alive
- Kill-take-a-safety

Diagram 21-4. An example of a kill-the-clock play call chart

CHAPTER 22
PLANNING A HAIL-MARY OFFENSE

In unsought-after circumstances, the offensive coordinator has found himself in a desperate situation. The game clock has a few seconds remaining. The offensive coordinator's team is behind and desperately needs to score points to win, or tie, the game. A last-minute, Hail-Mary pass of the football into the end zone, with the hope of it being caught by one of his receivers is the goal. In reality, there's a bit more helpful, Hail-Mary football thinking that can be utilized to help pull out that last-minute, desperation catch and score.

The Hail-Mary Pass Play

The commonly known Hail-Mary pass play truly is a desperation pass of the football, more often than not, thrown into the end zone. Of course, the quarterback tries to best use his passing fundamentals in an attempt to throw a high, deep pass that drops into the end zone for a Hail-Mary catch. In reality, there actually is a bit more to the Hail-Mary pass play than just a desperation deep pass into the end zone, hopefully caught by one of the offense's receivers.

The Hail-Mary play is actually made up of the Hail-Mary formation call (left and right), the blocking call, and the actual Hail-Mary pass pattern itself as shown in the example detailed in Diagram 22-1.

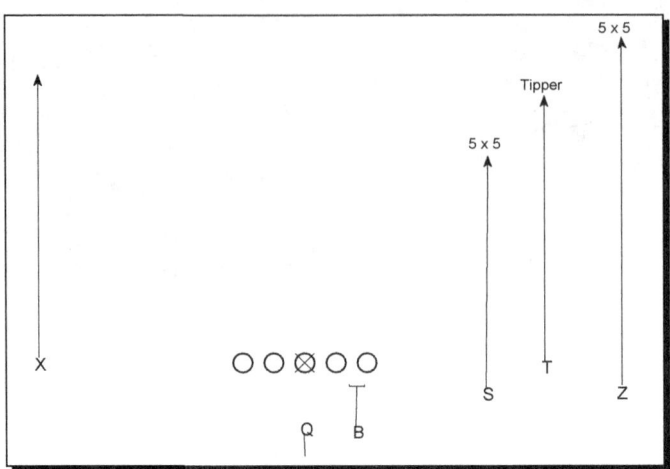

Diagram 22-1. An example of a Hail-Mary formation and play

In reality, the actual formation call is "Hail-Mary right" or "Hail-Mary left" or whatever left/right code words the offensive coordinator wants to utilize. The Hail-Mary right or left call is a three-by-one trips formation call, utilizing 10 personnel (four wide receivers). The combination of the tallest, speediest, and most athletic receiver on the offense should be the lead, point receiver, aligned in-between the widest and the tightest receivers of the trips formation.

The backside, single receiver ("X" in the diagram) runs a streak route. He is the first check by the quarterback to see what type of coverage the ("X") split end receiver is going to get. If the coverage to the backside is 1-on-1, the quarterback can then consider taking advantage of the 1-on-1 coverage with a deep streak route pass, especially if the cornerback coverage defender is not an exceptional player or not very deep. If the backside cover cornerback is an exceptional player and/or deep, the quarterback should stay to the three-receiver side.

The ("S") slot, ("T") tipper, and ("Z") flanker spread out to the trips side. The quarterback attempts to throw a deep pass into the end zone for the ("T") tipper, who is actually the prime receiver, to jump up in the air in an attempt to make the catch and score a touchdown.

If the ("T") tipper finds himself short of the goal line, he has two options. One option is to attempt to tip the football backwards over his outside shoulder to the widest ("Z") flanker receiver, who attempts to position himself five yards in width to the outside of and five yards deeper than the ("T") tipper. Hopefully, this five-by-five yard positioning alignment will be in the end zone, so that a catch of the tipped football to the ("T") tipper can result in a touchdown.

The second option for the ("T") tipper, once he realizes that a catch would probably not produce a touchdown, because he is not in the end zone, is to tip the football forwards and to the inside of the field to the trailing ("S") slot receiver, who is also in a five-by-five yard position alignment. The underlying premise in this scenario is to tip the football forwards to the trailing ("S") slot receiver, giving him a chance to catch the tipped football and run into the end zone for a touchdown.

The basic logic to this procedure is that the ("T") tipper is better off tipping the passed football backwards or forwards, if the tipper's catch would not occur in the end zone. Catching the football and trying to run for a touchdown into the end zone himself is not a reasonable option.

Supplemental Hail-Mary-Type Plays

While in this desperation situation, the offensive coordinator might look at the game clock and see 12 or 13 seconds on the clock or, possibly, a few more. This situation might just be enough time to execute one of two Hail-Mary disguised plays to get a chunk of 20 to 40 yards. Such a completion might help to put the offense in a great position for one, last, close-in throw or to attempt a field goal. On the other hand, the offense must make sure, upon completion of the pass, that the receiver catching and running with the football is able to get out of bounds to stop the clock. It is also important for the receiver to be aware that if he is able to make the catch inbounds for a needed first down, he must fall to the ground immediately to help the quarterback organize a quick pass to stop the clock for one, last play.

Diagram 22-2 illustrates the Hail-Mary package X-deep cross pass pattern that offers an excellent chance to quickly garner 25 to 40 yards either for one last pass into the end zone or for a field-goal attempt. It should be noted that the quarterback in the diagram is using dash, move-out pass-action. On the play, the quarterback should take a peek at the clearing streak routes, before scanning down to the X-deep cross route.

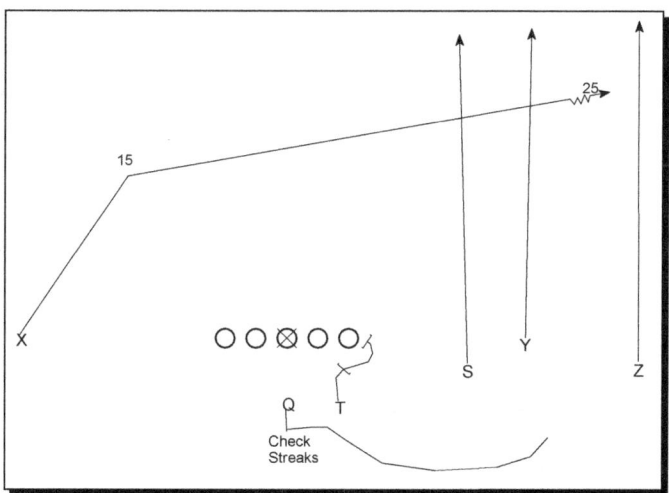

Diagram 22-2. Hail-Mary package X-deep cross pass pattern

Diagram 22-3 shows the Hail-Mary package ("S") slot-square out pass pattern that provides an excellent opportunity to quickly garner 18 to 25 yards either for one last pass into the end zone or for a field-goal attempt. This play is an exceptional pass-play concept with which to attack man-to-man coverage. On the play, the quarterback should check the deep, outside streaks, before scanning to the ("S") slot-square out route.

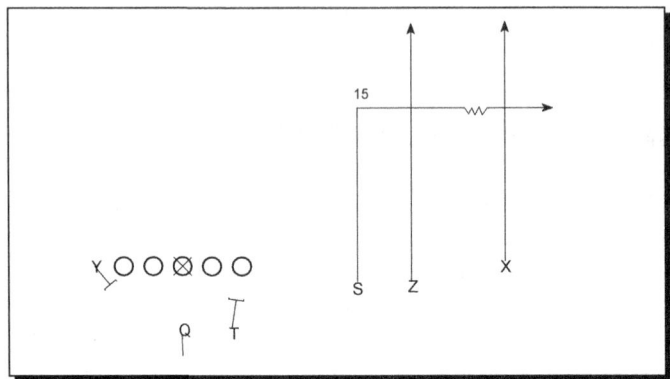

Diagram 22-3. Hail-Mary package ("S") slot square-out pass pattern

Diagram 22-4 illustrates the Hail-Mary package ("Z") and ("S") double square-out pass pattern that is similar to the ("S") slot square-out play. This pattern entails a sound pass play concept for attacking both zone and man-to-man coverages. On this play, the quarterback should check the deep, outside streak, before scanning down to the ("Z") flanker's square-out and then to the ("S") slot's square-out. The ("H") fourth receiver is shown to help stretch defensive coverages laterally and to provide a possible deep throw outlet.

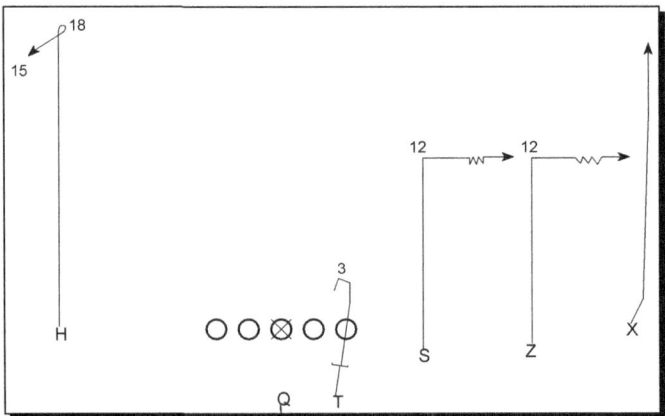

Diagram 22-4. Hail-Mary package ("S/Z") double square-out pass pattern

Diagram 22-5 provides an example of a Hail-Mary offense play call chart.

❐ Passes:
  • Hail-Mary
  • ("X") deep cross
  • ("S") slot square-out
  • ("S/Z") double square-outs

Diagram 22-5. Hail-Mary package play call chart

CHAPTER 23
FUNDAMENTALS—THE FOUNDATION OF AN OFFENSE

To this point, *The Offensive Coordinator's Football Handbook* has addressed a variety of relevant concepts for an offensive coordinator to consider. The book has gone from putting together an offensive staff to leadership and management to formulating red zone and goal line game plans to Hail-Mary desperation and scramble passing. And yet, it all still comes down to blocking and tackling, the building blocks for a sound, solid foundation upon which to build a football program. While offensive coordinators might not be overly concerned with tackling skills, they certainly are involved, every day, in an array of essential skills and techniques, such as blocking, passing, catching the ball, ballhandling, route running, ball security, and so forth.

In reality, someone could write a book of tremendous value concerning offensive and defensive fundamentals of the game of football alone. In fact, a number of such books have already been written. I would be remiss, however, if I didn't offer some key thoughts and insights concerning the teaching and coaching of offensive fundamentals that have served me well during the course of my career.

Constantly Stress the Teaching and Coaching of Fundamentals

No matter what type of offense you have—wishbone, triple-option, an I power offense, or a spread passing offense, every offense must have a strong, sound foundation on which it is built, if it is going to be successful. The proverbial well-built house will not stand for long, if the house's foundation is unsound and weak. The same factor is true for an offense. An offense can be multiple, sophisticated, and diverse. On the other hand, without basic fundamentals, such an offense will, most probably, have a tough time being consistently sound and effective. Just like the need for a rock-solid foundation for that house, an offense requires rock-solid fundamentals to be consistently successful.

When a discussion addresses rock-solid offensive fundamentals, it is referring to such skills as blocking, ball-carrying, passing, catching, ball security, and more. Doing a poor job of teaching and coaching any of these key fundamentals can lead to disaster. In fact, an entire chapter (Chapter 6) in this book has been devoted to the concept of "…what you do is important. However, how you do what you do is far more important!" How an offensive coordinator does what he does relates to how well he teaches and coaches the key fundamentals to his offense to help provide the foundation that it needs to be a winning and, hopefully, championship-level offense.

Constantly Coach the Hows and Whys of Correct Performance

Practice drills should focus on the hows and the whys of correct performance. This factor is true, whether such fundamental efforts are being executed well or when they need improvement. Furthermore, such feedback from the coach to the player must definitely be concise and to the point, with regard to what portions of a fundamental skill are being performed correctly and which require specific correcting.

The offensive coordinator must be demanding with regard to requiring correct performance at all times and that message must constantly be passed down to the assistant coaches and the players, as well. It is important for the assistant coaches to know that they are responsible for their players' mistakes and that the offensive coordinator will not tolerate excuses from either the assistant coaches or the players with regard to poor performance.

Equally important, the offensive coordinator expects his assistants to exhibit and create a positive learning environment when they're working with the players. For example, telling a player, or players, that their run blocking skills are "…terrible…" or that they "…stink…" does little, if anything, to help correct poor performance. Furthermore, he should stress the fact that "yelling" is not teaching.

First of all, a player must thoroughly know and understand what he is supposed to do and why he is supposed to execute his fundamentals in a specific way. For example, "Your stance base is much too wide, causing you to take a false, backward step on that block, John. Shorten your stance slightly, so you can comfortably step to your blocking target with the power of your body over that short, controlled step." Or, "…get your back elbow up, Eddie, when you hit your back, plant foot on your dropback action. When you tuck your elbow into your body, you tilt your front shoulder upward making your pass fly high." Such verbiage is what a player should hear, not that his performance "…stinks!"

Start Corrections With What the Players Do Right

Whenever an offensive coordinator can, he should always start his player's performance corrections with what his player did right. For example, "Nice, quick, 45-degree, take-off step, John. Now bring up your back foot just as explosively to immediately reform your blocking foot base. That will allow you to strike your hand blocking blows with power and a flat back."

Such a small, but positive, start to the verbal correction can help a player to feel that he is on the right tract … that he has started correctly with his first step and at this point, simply, needs to focus on his second step, enabling him to deliver his blocking strike with power and efficiency. Such small chunks of verbal positivity can often help "grease the skids" for a player to perform the required skills properly. Videotaping players can also be helpful. When videotaped, the coach is able to teach, coach, and correct a particular player, which enables the player to actually see the mistakes and sound corrections being made.

Refuse to Let Players Make Mistakes

In reality, players are going to make mistakes on the practice field, as well as in games. There's no doubt about it. Of course, making such mistakes in practice is when an offensive coordinator would rather see such mistakes made, rather than in a game.

On the other hand, mistakes simply cannot be tolerated by the offensive coordinator or his assistant coaches. As such, whenever possible in practice, a coach should quickly and definitively point out any mistake that, when quickly fixed, could make a difference in that player's ability to execute properly. For example, "You overstepped on that zone block, Charlie." In that instance, he might follow-up by telling that offensive lineman that he needs to shorten his front, zone lead step, so that he can break upfield to the linebacker level, if the defensive lineman to his zone-block action disappears away from him.

Personally, I like to have one-, two-, or three-word corrections for my quarterbacks that carry a lot of weight in their ability to correct mistakes. For example, if I yell out "elbow" from the sideline, it tells the quarterback to avoid tucking in his back, throwing elbow tightly to his body. Tucking in action of the back elbow frequently forces a quarterback to sit on his back foot. Sitting on his back foot will often produce a high release of the pass that can sail over the head of the intended receiver.

On the other hand, I might simply yell out "chest!" when a pass the quarterback threw on an out route to the sideline didn't seem to have much needed speed and power on it. By saying "chest," I'm able to tell the quarterback to get extra speed on the football, when passing it, by driving the football with extra power from his chest.

When the offensive coordinator or assistant coach observes a mistake that needs to be adjusted with more than a quick word or two, it is advisable for the coach to pull that player out of the on-the-field lineup and give him the requisite corrections. Using video camera footage of a practice or a segment of a game can also be helpful. Such video footage can help a player visualize and thoroughly understand his mistakes. Such a technique can be an invaluable resource to help an offensive coordinator and his assistants correct specific problems with the play of their athletes.

All-in-all, a well-coached offense does not make many mistakes. Furthermore, it does not make any, or close to any, dumb mistakes. Dumb mistakes are just that… dumb! Fighting, unsportsmanlike contact, targeting, and chop blocking are penalties that an alert, attentive player normally won't make. When a player does make such a dumb mistake, penalty running at the next practice is what might be needed to get the errant player's attention.

Emphatically Coach Ball Security

Over the years, I've seen a number of coaches whose efforts to coach ball security was, simply, a shout out of "…hang on to the dang ball…," when a quarterback, running back, tight end, or wide receiver fumbled the football. In reality, there's a lot more to ball security than verbally ripping into a ballcarrier, when he does fumble.

Ball security starts with proper ball security techniques and fundamentals. A properly held football can utilize one of two football security techniques. The first is the "squeeze-under-the-armpit" technique with "no air" showing between the armpit and the football. The ballcarrier's index and middle finger should straddle the front tip of the football and squeeze the football into the ballcarrier's armpit. The elbow of the ball-holding arm should be wrapped tightly underneath the football to enclose the football securely between the armpit, the locking index and middle fingers, and the ballcarrier's tightly wrapped elbow.

The ballcarrier must be sure to not cover the front tip of the football with his index finger. Such positioning of the index finger over the tip of the football can expose the index finger to being smashed by a direct hit from a defender, forcing the ball to be jarred loose. In addition, the ballcarrier can end up with an injured index finger from the index finger's collision with the defender, especially when it's a direct helmet hit.

As has previously been noted, there are two proper techniques to carrying a football. The second technique is the "high-and-tight" ball security technique. When the high-and-tight technique is utilized, the football is held with the same finger lock technique and the same, underneath elbow squeeze. The big difference is that with the high-and-tight technique, the football is held up high, with the front of the running back's chest pressing against the lower portion of the ballcarrier's shoulder pads.

Which of the two ball security holds is best? Arguably, I think they are very close to being an equal, e.g., "six of one and a half dozen of the other." The high-and-tight technique became popular with the increased efforts to strip the football from a ballcarrier's hold of the football, when the football was held directly under the ballcarrier's armpit. When held under the ballcarrier's armpit, the rear portion of the football can be exposed, which can enable a defender to punch the football out from behind.

Personally, if I had to choose between the two ball security hold techniques, I would use the "squeeze-under-the-armpit" technique, because, in my opinion, when the football is squeezed underneath the armpit with its three-point hold of the football, it is still well secured from a punch from the rear. In addition, I feel the ballcarrier can run more fluidly and quickly, when the "squeeze-under-the-armpit" technique is utilized.

In the opposite vein, I worry about the football being pressed hard up against the plastic of the shoulder pads, when employing the "high-and-tight" technique. The plastic of the shoulder pads is not pliable or soft to the pressuring hold of the football, making it more susceptible to squirting out from underneath the hand hold of the football upon contact. Furthermore, holding the football high-and-tight does not allow for as fluid or quick of a ballcarrier's running technique.

There is a third football-hold technique that is one that I would not personally recommend—the folding-arms technique, which is often used in a short-yardage situation for the purpose of good ball security. In reality, this technique is the weakest way to try to securely run with the football. In the folding-arms technique, the football is held laterally from side-to-side across the chest of the ballcarrier. As such, the ballcarrier crosses his arms in a "folding" manner, with his two hands cup-holding each end of the football. All factors considered, the folding-arms technique is the slowest of the three techniques, when it comes to running. The factor that worries me the most, however, is that if a defender rips upward on one elbow or the other, the football can easily be jarred-out from beneath the ballcarrier's folded arms.

One last, key ball-carrying technique is to have a ballcarrier carry the football in his outside arm, away from the heavy, inside-out flow of the defense's front defenders. As a result, a ballcarrier, running the football to the left on a sweep play, for example, should carry the football under his left, outside arm. Such ball-carrying action allows the ballcarrier, by using his body as a shield, to protect the football from the brunt of the defense's inside-out flow of, potentially, ball-striping/tackling defenders. In addition, the free, inside arm is able to rip upwards to help fend off such potential ball-strippers/tacklers.

The only problem with this body-shielding technique is that the football might end up in the ballcarrier's inside arm, if the running back pursues a cut-back run course. The key factor in this scenario is that no matter what arm the football is secured under, the ballcarrier should never attempt to switch the football to the opposite arm during the course of the football-carrying action. Switching the hold of the football from under one arm to the other leaves the football in an extremely, insecure position, which the defense can easily exploit to cause a big-time, ball-strip fumble.

CHAPTER 24
PRACTICING THE OFFENSE TO WIN

Practicing the offense, just as with planning the offense, is the responsibility of the offensive coordinator. The offensive coordinator is in charge of the team's seasonal, offensive practice efforts. It is his job to teach, and coach, with the big picture of the offense constantly in mind.

The underlying objective is for the football staff to teach great and coach great. To achieve such a goal, the offensive coordinator and his assistant coaches must be well-prepared for every practice, be it a grueling, full-padded contact-type practice or a light, no-padded, review practice the day before a game. No matter what the emphasis of the practice, the offensive coordinator should constantly be looking for better and more effective ways to motivate, teach, and coach.

Pre-Practice Teaching and Correction Meetings

Pre-practice teaching and correction meetings help to mentally provide the offensive players with essential football-related information that is needed to execute their play assignments to a point where they can be successful come game time. Such pre-practice and correction meetings are the settings for a coach to teach what he needs to teach, as well as coach what he needs to coach. It is an opportunity to have his players actually see and visualize what they must do on the field of play to become successful. A number of instructional tools can enhance the productivity of such meetings. For example, the use of dry boards (e.g., drawings and writings), instructional notes (read together as one offensive group), and video teaching presentations provide excellent teaching and coaching resources in a classroom setting.

Offensive meetings are a setting in which the players' questions can be brought forth. It is the time for the coaches to answer the players' questions, as well as explain the play concepts that are so important come game time. In addition, pre-practice teaching and correction meetings help alleviate the need for excessive talking and demonstrating on the practice field, when quality, physical practice repetitions are so essential. As a result, talking and explaining should be undertaken primarily during the offense's pre-practice meetings. Practicing on the practice field is designed for a quantity of quality repetitions with short, quick admonitions, when errors are made, and for positive words of support when correct, effective performances are displayed.

Walk-Through and Chair Drills

Walk-through drills are, in essence, meetings in which the players are on their feet, as they walk through alignments and play assignments to practice what is to be utilized in game-settings. Such walk-through drills can be held most anywhere there is enough physical space to accommodate all of a team's offensive players, e.g., the school's gymnasium, the wrestling room, the football field, or a parking lot.

The underlying consideration, with regard to walk-through drills, is that players are compelled to show their knowledge, or lack thereof, concerning their all-important, game-performance assignments. Simply stated, walk-through drills force the players to pay attention to a much greater degree than pre-practice, classroom meetings, during which the coach generally has difficulty assessing the amount of mental focus being put forth. This factor is especially true, when the lights are turned off to watch video-type presentations.

Another positive of walk-through drills is that during the check of players' assignments, the players are not being stressed physically, as they are during more normal, physical practices. As valuable as walk-through drills are to help check assignment needs, they are far less taxing on the body physically.

Whenever I felt that one of my offenses was acting fatigued and yet needed assignment and execution checks, I would start out the practice with 20 minutes of walk-throughs, allowing the players to take off their helmets and shoulder pads. For Saturday college-game days, I would take the offensive players outside into the parking lot before breakfast and undertake a relatively brief 10- to 12-minute session of walk-through drills, in an effort to finalize our blocking schemes and blitz-control assignments. On the other hand, if I felt we were facing a defense that produced a multitude of problems, the walk-through could last for up to 25 to 30 minutes. In fact, whenever we had extra walk-throughs and/or spent extra time on our walk-through practices, our offense quickly picked up on the importance of blocking and blitz controlling the opponent's defensive schemes.

One key for using walk-through drills is to have the players exaggerate their fundamentals as they "walk through." For example, a backside pulling guard does not stand straight up and down and walk/jog and play one-hand touch with the defensive end he is assigned to kick-out block. Instead, he should pull, with deep steps off the line of scrimmage, to take an inside-out course through the defensive end to enact the kick-out block action. As the pulling guard closes in on the defensive end, he should widen his stance, drop his hips, and exaggerate delivering an inside-out block, with exaggerated hand punches properly striking the defender. In turn, the quarterback should drop back into a slightly bent stance, with proper knee bend and body lean. He should go through the action of scanning his reads from side to side on a lateral read pass pattern and properly execute a high, over-the-head pass release. As such, each position on the offense should exaggerate their fundamentals as precisely as possible as the player "walks through" the offense's run and pass plays.

Another interesting practice concept is the chair drill. A chair drill simply involves lining up seating chairs for the offensive players, arranged in whatever formation the offensive coordinator wants to get the run and pass plays practiced. The chair drill gets the offensive players off their feet, helping to provide last-minute rest. During the chair drill, the players point out their blocking, run-and-pass play assignments, once the quarterback shouts out the play-call signal sent to him by the sideline, signal-caller coach.

The chair drill is an assignment-check drill. The offensive players must call out their blocking calls, as they point out their assigned defender to be blocked. The running backs point to their assigned run hole. The receivers point out their run-block or pass-route assignments, as the quarterback points out his run-play and pass-read assignments.

Have Short, Sharp, Motivated Practices

Quality versus quantity is a big decision to be made when considering the amount of time allotted for practices. More often than not, practice time considerations are more at the whim of a team's head coach, rather than the offensive, defensive, or special team's coordinators. Personally, I favor short, sharp, motivated practices any day of the week.

Personally, I dislike long, drawn-out, draggy practices in which the players seem to hit a wall after a certain point, as practices start to become sluggishly drawn out. At such a point, the players seem to be more interested in just getting the practice over with, rather than working hard to get better. I believe in sharp, short, motivated, quality practices, first and foremost, over practices where coaches are exerting as much time pushing their players to practice hard and fast, as they are in the actual teaching and coaching their players. As such, the offensive coordinator should strive for lots of quality drill repetitions by his players and assistant coaches.

The offensive players, as well as the defensive and special team's players, must always know the tempo being utilized during any specific point of a practice. For example, what is the block of practice time for the inside run drill shown on the posted daily practice time? Is it full-go blocking against the scout squad? Is it thud work, in which the offense and the scout defense form up their blocks and block-shedding techniques and fundamentals? Or, is the drill to be executed in a walk-through, totally non-contact tempo? Understanding the tempo is important, because misunderstanding of the practice tempo of a drill can easily result in an injury, due to a lack of proper communication.

The on-the-field communication mechanics practice must be as game-like as possible on a well-marked, fully lined, practice football field. All personnel substituting must enter the field from the marked, sideline player area. Down-and-distance situations must be marked with down-and-distance chains by manned student managers or injured players.

Work Hard to Develop a Blue-Collar Work Ethic

The game of football is a collision sport. Its physicality is unquestioned. As such, to succeed as a football player, an individual must possess a significant measure of mental and physical toughness. Frankly, a player who cannot develop significant levels of such traits will, simply, not have much of a chance of succeeding on the gridiron.

Can an offensive coordinator help to develop increased levels of toughness in his players? I believe he can. He can help develop increased levels of mental and physical toughness by working his players hard in an effort to develop a strong, blue-collar work ethic. Such a blue-collar work ethic includes such concepts as toughness, durability, endurance, and a resilient, never-give-up mentality in a player's efforts to help his offense succeed.

An offensive coordinator should constantly instill in the minds of his offensive players to be the hitters, as opposed to the players getting hit. He must constantly talk and teach toughness and praise the tough, demanding efforts by his players on the practice field, as well as in actual games, whenever possible. While a number of players have been brought up to be tough mentally and physically in their family, home, school, and community environments, others have not. Those individuals who have experienced "toughness" in a variety of settings have truly learned to work hard in their efforts to succeed as students, athletes, and members of their communities.

Arguably, blue-collar work ethics can be developed in those individuals who have never been taught the importance of getting dirty and rolling up their sleeves to achieve realistic, hard-earned, personally important goals. In that regard, tough conditioning drills and fast paced, hard-working individual, unit, and offensive team drills can help individual offensive players to fully understand that winning often comes at an extremely high price.

A well-conditioned, well-trained offensive football player takes pride in his hard-earned skills and his expended efforts to help his offense and his team to be consistent winners. Tough, hard-nosed, blue collar-type players earn the right to feel confident and be proud that they "gave it their all" on both the practice field and the game field come game day. On the other hand, the offensive coordinator must come to grips with the fact that there will always be some players who will not show, or exhibit, characteristics of toughness, determination, and grit and, quite possibly, never will.

Demand Hustle!

No matter what the tempo of a specific drill, loafing can never be allowed. Hustle must be the bottom line essence of every practice. As such, the offensive coordinator and his assistants must demand effort—hard-working, hustling, never-ending effort at all times on the practice field.

During practice, each group of offensive players should sprint from one drill to the next. On a practiced run play, the ballcarrier should be taught to burst for a minimum of 10 yards past the line of scrimmage and, then, be sure to jog back to the huddle, with the football securely tucked under his football carrying arm. This approach helps promote the mindset of a constantly hard-working offense that exhibits a sustained pattern of all-out effort that reflects an absolute habit for the way all things are done by the offense. Coaching for quality and coaching short, sharp motivated practices are concepts that go hand-in-hand.

There's No Substitute for Freshness

"There's no substitute for freshness!" was a phrase that was drilled into our coaches over and over again, when I was on the Wildcat's staff, by our head coach, Larry Smith at the University of Arizona. This concept also went hand-in-hand with Larry's emphasis on "short, sharp, motivated practices." In reality, working his players hard as an offensive coordinator is an excellent concept, as long as he's not wearing his players out.

If an offensive coordinator owned quality, thoroughbred race horses, I doubt he would run them into the ground in their conditioning efforts directly before a race. Instead, he would, over time, build them up to a peak condition and then gradually cut back to make sure his thoroughbreds were well-rested and in a top-speed form in an effort to win their races.

In reality, peaking an offensive coordinator's players to top condition at game time is no different than tapering off the training efforts of those thoroughbred horses. Having tough, driving, intense practices on a Monday and a Tuesday for a Friday night game and then tapering off the time and intensity of the team's practicing on Wednesday and Thursday is a normal coaching and training regimen. On the other hand, when three-quarters of the season is over, the offensive coordinator might find that his offensive players seem to be running on "flat, or somewhat deflated, tires."

What does an offensive coordinator do when he feels that his players have tired legs and bodies? The straightforward answer is that he should cut back. For example, he could have the offensive players spend 15 extra minutes in the meeting room watching video-game tapes of their next opponent. Or, he could devote the first 20 minutes of his practices to performing walk-through drills.

One drill I liked to utilize for the first 10 to 15 minutes of practice for later-week practice days was a "fix-it" drill. A fix-it drill focused on walking through a script of the dozen or so offensive plays that they seemed to have had trouble with during the first few days of a game-practice week. Such drills as a walk-through drill or a fix-it drill or, simply, extended videotape viewing of an upcoming opponent can be of tremendous value to the offense's performance, while allowing their legs and bodies to get some needed rest. Some offensive coordinators (probably more head coaches) will, simply, cut back on the total length of practices as the season starts to wind down. Whatever the method utilized, the phrase, "there's no substitute for freshness" is a concept with which all coaches should abide.

Compete, Compete, Compete …But, Be Careful!

Compete, compete, compete! Whenever players practice, competition is a great motivator for the individuals involved. For example, when a cornerback works to cover a wide receiver, who is trying to run a proper route and make a reception, there, normally, is a great sense of competition between the offensive and defensive players. The same factor is true when an offensive lineman and a defensive lineman compete in a one-on-one pass rush/pass block drill.

Such highly competitive drills can, then, be built upon to larger and larger degrees. For example, a live three-on-three run block drill pitting three offensive linemen versus three defensive linemen, with a football under the arm of a running back behind the offensive blockers, is an extremely popular, competitive, offense-versus-defense drill. Of course, coordinators can stretch competitive drills to such drills as 7-on-7 pass drills and, even, live, full-team scrimmages. More often than not, the intensity exhibited in such competitive drills is an accurate barometer of who a team's true competitors actually are. As such, an offensive coordinator should just watch those drills, and he'll quickly see his most competitive players competing intensely.

The concern for competitive practice drills that contain an extended number of players is that the greater the number of players involved in full, live-type drills, the greater the chances of injuries occurring. On occasion, such drills end up producing injuries, due to the tangling of feet and legs or the falling of players on the legs of other players.

Be Concerned About Live, Full-Go Scrimmage Work

I coached for three years under coach Homer Smith, while on the staff at the United States Military Academy at West Point. The cadet players were amazing individuals as people, students, soldiers, and football players.

Our primary problem was that few of our players were of top, major-college caliber. The top, major college recruits, for the most part, had it in their minds that they were going to the NFL upon graduation, rather than serving in the Army for, at the time, four years of military commitment. While we had some excellent players at Army, they were often fewer in number than the teams we played.

While Coach Smith demanded that our assistant coaches help our players to develop tough, hard-nosed football players, he was well-aware that we did not have a lot of quality, Division I players and that we needed to try to keep as many of those quality players as we could healthy. As a result, we practiced almost all of our competitive, live drills on a one-on-one basis. For example, our running backs would practice live-cut blocking drills against our defensive ends one-on-one. Offensive linemen run-blocked defensive linemen one-on-one. The same offensive-versus-defensive line drill was utilized for pass protection.

Why the one-on-one format? We would utilize live, one-on-one, offensive-versus-defensive drills to prevent the "stacking of bodies" that often occurs when offenders and defenders fall on one another in live contact drills involving multiple players. A two-on-two or three-on-three blocking drill doubles, or triples, the possibility of "stacking" bodies and the enhanced likelihood of possible injuries. This factor was the reason that, while at West Point, we never practiced live, scrimmage work. I have coached on staffs where we had a multitude of live, full-team practice scrimmages. Unfortunately, as a part of such programs, I've also seen four, five, and six players standing on the sideline, out for the rest of the season, as a result of injuries that occurred during such full-team scrimmage work.

It should be remembered, however, is that live, physical, full-contact drills that pit offensive and defensive players against one another are not without value. In fact, live pass-protection blocking of two adjacent offensive blockers versus two adjacent defensive linemen when the defenders are practicing twist stunts can be great, game-like, practice work. On the other hand, utilizing a live offensive pass protection/defensive line twist stunt drill, with five offensive line blockers and four twisting/stunting defensive linemen, can more than double the possibility of injuries.

As such, an offensive coordinator should limit, or isolate, such full-team, full-contact drills, into the smallest of personnel groupings needed to get the practice work effectively accomplished. For example, the half-line scrimmage drill illustrated in Diagram 24-1 shows half of the offensive front personnel being pitted against half of the defensive front personnel, working against one another in a live, half-scrimmage type setting. In fact, the drill could be set up with the stipulation of only being able to wrap the running back up, as opposed to tackling him to the ground, to help protect the running back from injury.

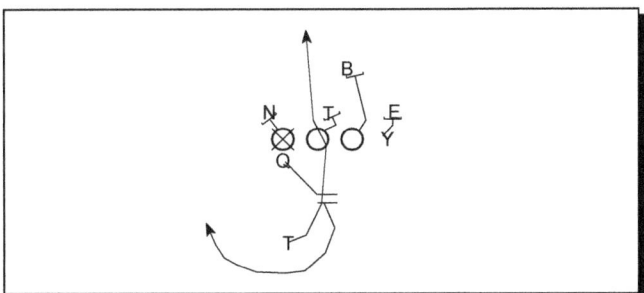

Diagram 24-1. Half-line scrimmage drill

If and when the offensive coordinator (or the head coach) decides to full-team scrimmage, such scrimmages should be organized, once again, around the concept of short, sharp, motivated, full-scrimmage work. Some coaches prefer to have one, two, or even three long scrimmages. The problem with such long scrimmages is that an extended number of scrimmage repetitions can lead to tired players. As a rule, tired players can more easily be injured.

Personally, I like having one medium-long, full-go scrimmage that takes place 10 or 11 days before the team's first game of the season. The 10-day intermission between that final scrimmage and the team's first game of the season is extremely important from a freshening-up standpoint. Beyond the one, longer scrimmage could be a series short scrimmages, worked into normal, daily practice schedules. For example, a 12- to 16-play goal line scrimmage could be one such short scrimmage. A relatively brief, 16-play, third-down scrimmage could be another. Four series (two by the first team and two by the second team) of a red zone scrimmage is another extremely viable possibility. Even a short coming-out scrimmage or a short two-minute scrimmage could be of great assistance to the development of a team's offense and defense. The point to remember is that short, mini-scrimmages of such strategic, game-like situations help to sharpen the excitement of more normally organized, daily practices.

Practice With Game-Like Specificity

Much of this book has been based on the concept of game-like specificity. Such specificity focuses on the teaching and coaching of the skills of the game of football necessary to succeed as an offense. The underlying premise of such skills is to move the football closer and closer to the opponent's goal line, until the football crosses the goal line, resulting in a touchdown.

Personally, I believe that an offensive coordinator should design his practices based on a team's offensive playbook, not some football drill book. Far too often, some coaches utilize practice drills that seem to have little to do with practicing the skills necessary to execute their offensive run and pass plays.

In reality, there are a number of football coaching books about practice drills that can be extremely helpful in helping a coordinator practice the skills needed to be successful come game time. Arguably, however, an offensive coordinator would be best served by creating his own drills that can help his team to execute the requisite skills of his offensive plays. For the most part, his drills should simply practice dissected portions of his offense, so that his players actually practice in a more game-like manner.

Diagram 24-2 illustrates a game-like situation, sprint-out pass drill. In the drill, the quarterback executes his sprint-out action with three different variations. In the first sprint-out action, the quarterback rolls-out (shown by the solid line) and then turns up to run directly at the pass net target 12-yards deep (representing a comeback-out) and four to five yards from the sideline. This sprint-out action is the basic, running sprint-out action, in which the quarterback bends up toward the line of scrimmage, running at the pass target.

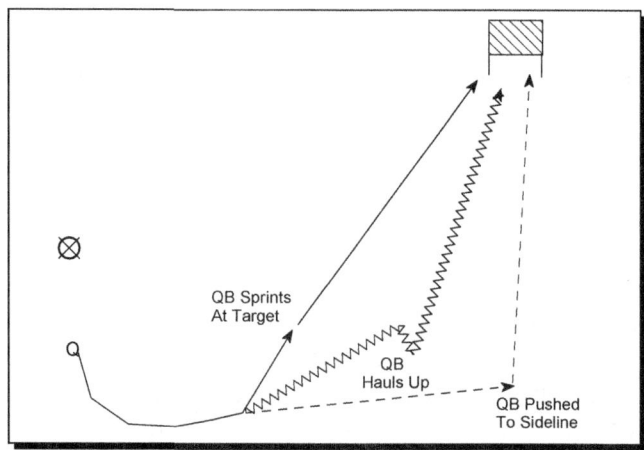

Diagram 24-2. Sprint-out pass drill

In the second sprint-out action (detailed by the dotted line), the quarterback flattens-out his course in an effort to avoid a close pursuing defensive pass rusher, who is trying to cutoff the quarterback's run path toward the line of scrimmage. When the quarterback flattens his run-action outwards toward the sideline, he no longer has the run advantage helping him to square-up his run throwing-action to the passing target. As a result, the quarterback needs to follow-through to a greater degree with his throwing hand to the passing target, as he runs toward the sideline.

In the third sprint-out action (conveyed by the wavy line), the quarterback is shown hauling-up and setting his feet due to defensive pressure from the outside, executing a non-running, down-the-field throw action. The coach, in this drill, mixes up these sprint-out actions and also varies the passing targets to represent curl-route throws, post-corner routes, comeback-out routes, and deep streak routes. Such an offensive drill is definitely a game-like, situational offensive drill that comes directly from a team's playbook, as opposed to a drill book.

Intently Practice Sideline-to-Field Play Call Communications

One of the most overlooked practice concepts involves the issue of personnel substitution usage, player substitutions, and play-call communications. All of the hard work of practicing a run or a pass can all go for naught, if such sideline communications are not air tight and efficiently executed. To properly implement the mechanics of such sideline communications, the sideline signal callers should be coaches, even though many teams utilize substitute players.

Signaled calls must be expedient and, yet, not act rushed. They must be clearly understood so that there is absolutely no miscommunication—no flubbed or missed calls or checks, even if the plays are carried in by substitutes or are a part of wristband, play-listing reading. Plays must not be sent in incorrectly. Furthermore, there must never be a delay-of-game penalty due to breakdowns of play-call communication.

The communication mechanics practice must be as game-like as possible on a well-marked, fully lined football field. All personnel substituting must enter the field from the marked, sideline player area. Down-and-distance situations must be marked with down-and-distance chains and markers, manned by student managers or injured players.

Make Teaching/Coaching Training Videos

The use of the videotaping of practice drills or instructional training video tapes made from actual game videos is about as good a teaching/coaching tool as a coach can utilize in helping his players to see, and understand, incorrect and correct performance. Legendary NFL coach Jim McNally is one of the finest offensive line coaches I have ever known. One year, in the mid-1980s, my offensive line coach and I visited Jim at the Cincinnati Bengals' training facility. After initial pleasantries, Jim asked what he could do for us. We were interested in finding out about his zone blocking techniques. Jim quickly said, "Let's go down to our offensive line meeting room, and I'll get you fixed up."

When we entered the offensive linemen's room, we saw a long, meeting room table with equally long metal, file racks, filled with 16-millimeter teaching and training films. (Videotapes were still a long way from being developed.) Jim grabbed a film can from the middle of the pack and went into an excellent discourse of zone run blocking, supported by his teaching/coaching/training films.

"How about the zone blocking of defensive line twists, Jim?," I remember asking. Jim simply went to a different part of the film racks and pulled out another excellent teaching/coaching/training film. Back then, creating such teaching and coaching films was expensive and time-consuming. Today, computer-editing machines can whip up such excellent teaching/coaching/training videos in a matter of minutes.

CHAPTER 25
BE SURE TO ENJOY THE JOURNEY

When a coach takes on the role of offensive coordinator, he takes on a lot of responsibility. When the team wins, the offensive coordinator usually is able to bask in the sun, and often receives pats on the back from the head coach. Of course, the team might have won due to an excellent performance by the defense, with all the plaudits going to the defensive coordinator.

In reality, when a coach becomes the offensive coordinator, the offensive "buck" starts and ends with him. What the offense is, or is not, able to do comes under the charge of the offensive coordinator. The offensive coordinator will, ultimately, be responsible for the effectiveness of the offense. Hopefully, the offensive coordinator will relish the many challenges, big and small, that he will face with a sense of excitement, enjoyment, and empowerment.

There certainly can be factors that impact the performance of an offense that the offensive coordinator cannot control, both good and bad. For example, injuries can be a devastating factor, when a large number of players can be lost for the season or be out for a considerable amount of games. In reality, the head coach might be an individual who has a lot to say about his offense, which could be good or bad for the offensive coordinator. On the other hand, the offensive coordinator could be blessed with a tremendous, passing quarterback, as well as a load of superfast, quality wide receivers. That's the good news. The bad news is that the offensive talent on the junior varsity and freshmen teams is at an all-time low.

What is the message in this instance? The message is that an offensive coordinator never truly knows what's going to happen, once his offense takes the field of play for its first game of the season. That freshmen group of players might mature to be an extremely effective group of offensive players. Conversely, the star quarterback the offensive coordinator had might get hurt in the last scrimmage the team had before the first game of the season and be out for the year. In reality, no matter how much an offensive coordinator thinks he has his offense in control, one or two factors might suddenly arise to positively, or negatively, affect the quality of his offense.

What can he do, as the offensive coordinator, when such good or bad factors or situations arise? One thing he can do is to build an offense that has the ability to be flexible. For example, if his starting quarterback is a tremendous, pro-style passing quarterback, but his second string quarterback is a good run-option type quarterback, he better have an offense that can flip-the-switch easily from one style of play to another, without undue difficulty.

The wing-T offense has been around for a long time, especially on the high school level. Why is the wing-T offense still so popular on the high school level? Because, it has the ability to easily "juice-up" the wing-T's pass game, if the offensive coordinator finds out that he has an excellent, passing, junior quarterback who will be around for two years. In the same vein, the wing-T has the ability to easily "juice-up" the run-option portions of the wing-T offense, if the second-team, run-option quarterback has to suddenly go out onto the field to lead the offense.

Be a Great Offensive Coordinator

Being an offensive coordinator is generally a tough, year-round job. There are so many aspects to the role that many an offensive coordinator have wondered how they're going to get all of their workload done. Effective, year-long, organization is certainly an important key. Proper, effective, delegation is another.

The major key to being a great offensive coordinator is to relentlessly work to be the boss of the offense…the leader…the manager. Being the offensive coordinator is a phenomenal job. It involves a phenomenal responsibility, as well as a phenomenal challenge. The position entails an exceptional level of responsibility and challenge, because as a high school offensive coordinator, he's dealing with a large group of young men in the age range of 15 to 18 years old who must be molded into a cohesive group. On the college level, the age range is, on the average, from 18 to 23 years old. In addition, he will have a staff, small or large, to lead and manage.

The offensive coordinator is the boss of the offense. Like it or not, what happens on the game field, offensively, comes under his charge. It should also be noted that he is one of the few coaches on the staff who can proudly and excitedly command and lead a major portion of the team—in this instance, the offense.

Without question, every offensive coordinator should strive to do his job to the best of his ability. Just as he demands the best of his offensive players and assistant coaches, he should demand a hard-working, blue-collar work ethic of himself. In reality, with the exception of the head coach, no other coach on the staff commands more of the possible results of the team's success.

The offensive coordinator should hate to lose as much as he loves to win. As such, he should strive daily, weekly, monthly, and yearly to help make his offense the best it can be. Then, when the season is over, he should reflect and evaluate to immediately start off a new season with even greater passion and determination than he did in the last.

The Importance of Having Fun

No matter how the offense plays and practices, the offensive coordinator should be sure to have fun, both personally and with his fellow coaches. His colleagues are the combatants-in-arms with whom he will interlock his arms to teach and coach the young men he so passionately works to develop. While football coaching can certainly be a tough, pressure-packed profession, when coaches are asked why they coach, they will often state, "because it's my passion."

Winning is joyous, exhilarating, and tremendously satisfying. Losing is none of those. Still, coaching football, as an offensive coordinator, can be an obsessive undertaking that makes the individual want for more and more. It can also entail a rough, demanding journey. In reality, that journey could also be the reason that a person lives for the role—the challenge…the excitement…the satisfaction.

The bottom line is that an individual should enjoy being an offensive coordinator. It's a journey that can make a worthwhile difference in the lives of others, as well as in himself.

ABOUT THE AUTHOR

Steve Axman was, most recently, the quarterbacks coach for the Arizona Hotshots of the Alliance of American Football for Head Coach Rick Neuheisel in 2019. In 2018, he was the offensive coordinator and quarterbacks coach for the Arizona Rattlers of the Indoor Football League, as well as the quarterbacks coach for Perry High School in Gilbert, AZ. At Perry, Axman coached quarterback Brock Purdy, two-time Arizona 6A Player of the Year. Prior to that, Axman served as the interim head coach at Nicholls State University for the 2014 season and quarterbacks coach at Simon Fraser University in Burnaby, Canada (2013). Prior to that, he was the assistant head coach and offensive coordinator at the University of Idaho (2007-2011), quarterbacks coach at the University of Montana (2006), and wide receiver coach at the University of Washington, a position he assumed before the 2004 season. It was Axman's second stint on the Huskies staff. Previously, he served as the assistant head coach and quarterbacks coach. While at Washington, Axman oversaw the work of record-setting quarterbacks Marques Tuiasosopo and Cody Pickett. During the 2003 season, he was the offensive coordinator and quarterbacks coach at UCLA.

Axman is no stranger to wide-open, multiple offense football or for producing top-flight collegiate quarterbacks. During his career, he has worked at four Pac-10 schools (UCLA, Arizona, Stanford, and Washington). Among his former collegiate pupils are Troy Aikman, Matt Moore, and Drew Olsen (UCLA), Neil O'Donnell (Maryland), Jeff Lewis and Travis Brown (Northern Arizona), and Tom Tunnicliffe (Arizona).

In 1998 (prior to joining the UW staff the first time), Axman served as the quarterbacks coach at Minnesota. Before that, Axman was the head coach at Northern Arizona from 1990-97. He inherited a NAU program that had experienced just three winning seasons during the 1980s, and had never qualified for the Division 1-AA post-season playoffs. During his eight years with the Lumberjacks, Axman guided the team to a 48-41 record. making him the second winningest coach in Northern Arizona's history.

Axman's NAU teams were known for their offensive fireworks. During his eight-year career, Axman's teams averaged 30 points per game. His 1996 Lumberjack squad set or tied 14 national records, averaging 42.3 points per game en route to a 9-3 overall record and a 6-1 record in the Big Sky Conference. That season produced a second-place finish in the Big Sky, the school's first post-season appearance, and a school-best No. 6 national ranking. For that 1996 season, tailback Archie Amerson won the Walter Payton Award for his record 2,079 yards of rushing. In 1989, Axman served as the quarterbacks coach for Maryland, where he worked with O'Donnell. In 1987-88, he was the offensive quarterbacks coach at UCLA, where he coached Aikman. Interestingly, O'Donnell (Steelers) and Aikman (Cowboys) faced off against one another as the two starting quarterbacks in Super Bowl XXX.

Prior to UCLA, Axman coached at Stanford (1986), with the Denver Gold of the United States Football League (1985), and at the University of Arizona (1980-1984), as the offensive coordinator and quarterbacks coach. Axman previously spent a year at Illinois, three seasons at Army, and one season at Albany State. Before that, Axman's first collegiate coaching assignment was at East Stroudsburg University in 1974. A 1969 graduate of C.W. Post College in Greenvale, NY, Axman went on to earn his first master's degree from Long Island University in 1972 and his second in 1975, while coaching at East Stroudsburg University.

Axman has authored 15 instructional books on football coaching. He has also been featured on seven well-received instructional videos on football coaching. He is nationally renowned for this knowledge of offensive fundamentals, schemes, and techniques, particularly quarterback play.

A native of Long Island, NY, Axman and his wife, Dr. Marie Axman, a retired elementary school principal, have four daughters: Mary Beth, Jaclyn, Melissa, and Kimberly, as well as five grandchildren.

Books by Steve Axman*

- *The Offensive Coordinator's Football Handbook*
- *101 Concepts for a Successful Football Program*
- *Coaching the Quick Pass Game*
- *Offensive Game and Practice Planning for Winning Football*
- *101 Concepts for Effective Football Practice*
- *Attacking Coverages With the Passing Game*

- *101 Concepts for Effective Offense*
- *Coaching Critical Situation Offense*
- *Coaching Offensive Backs*
- *Coaching Quarterback Passing Mechanics*
- *101 Dropback Pass Patterns*
- *101 Quarterback Drills*
- *The Complete Handbook of Offensive Football Drills*
- *Attacking Modern Defenses With the Multiple-Formation Veer Offense*
- *The Pro-Read Option Attack for Winning Football*

*Additional information on books written by Steve Axman is available at www. coacheschoice.com.